MAKING AN ANIMATED FILM
a practical guide

MATT WEST

CROWOOD

First published in 2005 by
The Crowood Press Ltd
Ramsbury, Marlborough
Wiltshire SN8 2HR

www.crowood.com

© Matt West 2005

British Library Cataloguing-in-Publication Data
A catalogue record for this book is available from the British Library.

ISBN 1 86126 724 X

Typeset by Jean Cussons Typesetting, Diss, Norfolk

Printed and bound in Great Britain by Biddles Ltd, King's Lynn

CONTENTS

ACKNOWLEDGEMENTS

This book is all about mistakes, or, to be more accurate, how to avoid making too many of them, and it wouldn't have been written without a great deal of help from a number of people who have tolerated and corrected my own errors.

First among these people is Steve Roberts, the best animation teacher I've ever encountered. I learned a huge amount from him while at the London Animation Studio, for which I shall be eternally grateful. I stopped being a student some time ago, but, as well as kidding myself that I still look like one, I try to remember that I'm still learning, and will be for as long as I'm animating. For this reason a great deal of thanks are owed to virtually everyone I've ever worked with, who have taught me all kinds of things without even being aware that they were doing so. A list of them could take up at least a couple of chapters but still risk leaving someone out, and so I hope that they're not offended by remaining nameless.

I should also thank mum, dad and my brother Chris for the superhuman effort required to keep the collective family jaw undropped when I announced that I'd decided to be an animator. Thanks are also due to my grandfather for providing welcome relief from animation with long conversations about cricket, and to my grandmother for suggesting that I should draw a black line around the people in my pictures to make them stand out. I was five at the time, but I'm still using the trick now.

Finally, a huge thanks to Rachael for all her support, and her continued, some would say biased, belief that I'm the best thing since sliced bread. I think she's pretty good too.

Matt West
summer 2004

1   INTRODUCTION

This book is aimed at anyone who is thinking of making his or her first animated film. If you have an idea for such a film and are not sure what to do, nor, indeed, what order to do it in, this book will guide you through all the stages you need to turn your idea into animated reality.

The reader is not expected to have any prior knowledge of the process of animation and so every effort has been made to explain all the details involved. This means that those readers who are already studying animation or working with it every day may find that some sections go over material already familiar to them. For this reason, the book has been written in a way which should allow readers to dip into the chapters relevant to them.

At this stage, it is worth making clear that the book is not intended to be an exhaustive guide to the craft of animation itself. There are already a number of excellent books covering this and listed in the Bibliography. The present aim, as the title suggests, is to focus on the practical – what you need to do, and when, to produce a finished animated film.

As a final note, it is worth remembering that, although the processes described represent the ideal way of making an animated film, we do not live in an ideal world. When working on a film it is all too easy to find yourself short of time and money, and, consequently, having to rush through some stages of film-making, or to start working on one stage before finishing the one before. Do not worry about this; some of the best animation has come from working with limited budgets in less than ideal circumstances. What is important is your final film; the book is intended as a guide to the best way of getting that film made; it is not a rule book which should be followed to the letter.

WHAT IS ANIMATION?

Animation is a trick played on the eye. When you look at a sequence of still images shown in quick succession, you can trick yourself and your audience into believing that they are seeing a moving image.

As we can see from the examples overleaf, you need many images in a short space of time for animation to successfully trick the eye. Most animated feature films will have twenty-four for each second of movement. Television series can get away with showing only twelve images per second (see Chapter 5 for more information on frame rates).

All these images mean that animation is not something which can be done quickly. Whatever form of animation you are doing you will have to create an image for every single frame of your film; although much of the work involved has been made faster by the use of computers, it remains a hugely time-consuming way of making a film. It is worth bearing this in mind as you begin making your animated film. It is also a good

When these drawings are shown over the space of ten frames (slightly less than half a second), the man appears to be walking.

idea to give some consideration as to how your own skills and interests fit in with animation as a whole. If you are someone who likes to spend a long time on every drawing or artwork you do, then it is likely that you will be better at and get more enjoyment from working on character design and backgrounds than the actual process of animation. If, on the other hand, you enjoy coming up with ideas for films, then you might be better suited to script writing.

Of course, when you are making your own animated film it is possible for you to do absolutely everything, from script and character design to voices and animation. However, you should not feel obliged to do everything on your own; animation often works best as a collaborative process and so if you know someone who is good at doing voices or have a friend whose paintings

would make perfect backgrounds try to get them involved too.

A BRIEF HISTORY OF ANIMATION

When making an animated film it is useful to have an idea of how the medium got started and evolved. The most important thing to understand is that animation is a very young art form. The first animated film was released only in 1906, with the first feature length film, Disney's *Snow White and the Seven Dwarfs* not coming out until 1937. When compared to the length of time people have been painting or writing, the lifespan of animation is short. It is, consequently, a much less stable and less well understood medium than these older art forms; people are still finding new ways of working and different techniques. For instance, the development of 3D computer animation packages in the last twenty years has produced a style of animation which would have been an impossibility when many of today's animators began their careers.

How Animation Began

Although the first animated films did not appear until the early 1900s, the idea of viewing sequential drawings to create the illusion of movement really started in the middle of the nineteenth century. Around this time several different ways of performing a basic version of the trick of animation were developed. The most familiar of these is the 'flipbook', a small book which can be flipped through at speed with your thumb.

People still play with flipbooks today, and they can be a good way of beginning to experiment with animation, especially as the small pad of paper you will need to make one is far cheaper than specialist animation paper.

Another early way of viewing moving drawn images was the zoetrope. This worked by placing a strip of drawings inside the zoetrope and then spinning it while watching the strip through the slits in the side. These slits concentrated the eye on the space the drawings were moving into rather than the movement of the whole strip, thus creating the illusion of movement. It is still possible to buy zoetropes and they are also fairly easy to make: all you need is a biscuit tin with evenly spaced slits cut into its side and a way of spinning it around a central point. When experiment-

A flip book, the simplest possible form of animation.

A zoetrope can be used to make looping animation.

ing with these original forms of animation remember that with the zoetrope you will need to produce an animation that loops; that is, the last drawing must lead back into the first one, since you will see your animation several times within one spin. With flipbooks, it is possible to create linear animation, where the end is different from the beginning.

The First Animated Films

At the same time that zoetropes and flip-books were gaining popularity, people were working on a way to create the illusion of live action movement, work which would lead to the invention of film. In 1896 one of those involved in this work, Thomas Edison, met the newspaper cartoonist James Stuart Blackton. Together they produced the first animated film, showing the changing expressions of a man and his wife; this was released in 1906 under the title *Humorous Phases of Funny Faces.*

However, it was Winsor McCay, another newspaper cartoonist, who really began to understand the potential of animation. He experimented with many different formats, including making films of his own comic strips (*Little Nemo in Slumberland*) and inter-acting with animated characters. McCay toured the USA speaking in front of his film *Gertie the Dinosaur*, talking to Gertie and even appearing to throw her an apple. Perhaps his most significant film was *The Sinking of the Lusitania*, made in 1918. This was the first animated film to tackle serious, dramatic, real life events and opened the eyes of many to the potential of animation.

Disney and the 'Golden Age'

One of these people was, of course, Walt Disney. In the early 1920s Disney began making animated films, and in 1928 made *Steamboat Willie*, the first animated film fully synchronized with sound (and the first to feature Mickey Mouse). The quantum leap which took him from this break-through to the production of *Snow White*, a feature length film in 1937, is nothing less than remarkable. Disney followed it with *Pinocchio*, and then with *Fantasia*, the com-bination of classical music and animation. By now Disney's company had become a production line for extraordinary anima-tion, making a new animated feature at least once a year and often more than that. Even the Second World War was powerless to stop their success since Disney simply shifted the focus away from European audi-ences towards South America, with *Saludos Amigos* and *The Three Caballeros*.

The period between the start of the Disney productions and the beginning of the 1960s is often referred to as the 'Golden Age' of animation. This is because, as well as the beginning of the Disney empire, the period saw the creation of all the classic, short animation films which many children are still brought up on today. The first Tom and Jerry film, created by William Hanna and Joseph Barbera, came out in 1940. At the same time, the Warner Brothers' *Looney Tunes* films, starring Bugs Bunny, Daffy Duck and others, were beginning. If all this was not enough, the great animation direc-tor Tex Avery was producing his incredible films for MGM, starring Droopy, often alongside a lecherous wolf and a pretty young girl named Red.

The Rise of Television Animation

It is no coincidence that nearly all the ani-mation seen as representative of the Golden Age was made for the cinema. (Short films such as *Looney Tunes* were shown before the main feature as part of a programme of films.) This meant that audiences were pay-ing directly to watch the animation, a situa-tion which changed drastically when television replaced cinema as the main way in which people watched cartoons. This led to much animation being funded by the smaller budgets provided by television sta-tions and advertising revenue, instead of the larger sums which came from ticket money.

This change in funding led to the depar-ture of Hanna and Barbera from MGM in 1957 to set up a new company, called, nat-urally, Hanna-Barbera, and specializing in animation for television. In 1960 they launched *The Flintstones*, the first really suc-cessful animated television series. However, as time and budgets grew shorter, Hanna-Barbera's output rarely managed to match this initial success, with the company becoming known for the cheap production values of its shows.

It is worth remembering the economic factors involved when looking at what many consider to be the decline of anima-tion after the early 1960s. Although it is easy to use the reduction in quality from, say, the original *Tom and Jerry* to the *Scooby Doo* series as evidence of a slump in the animators' ability, this is far from accurate. Indeed, in many cases the television series of the 1970s were being animated by the same animators who worked on the great successes of the 1940s and the 1950s, but working on a much tighter budget.

The rise of television created a hierarchy of animation that still exists today. The most money, and therefore the most lavish animation, is found in feature films. The second best financed strand of animation is found in commercials, for which individual companies are prepared to pay large sums to advertise their products. Finally, animation for television series is subject to the tightest budgets. Individual short films, such as the Oscar-winning *Wallace and Gromit* films by Aardman or the equally successful films by Bob Godfrey or Michael Dudok de Witt, exist in an uncertain space between these hierarchies. Such films are made for love not money, and any shortfalls in funding they may suffer are more than compensated for by the dedication and time put into them by their creators.

As the age of television entered the 1980s, for the first time in its short life animation began to settle down. No one had managed to successfully challenge Disney's status as the foremost producer of animated features, and Disney itself had started to become formulaic, relying on a traditionally successful mix of stock characters and songs to provide it with its accustomed success. By now, a traditional canon of animation had been built up, including all the Disney successes alongside *Tom and Jerry* and the *Looney Tunes* films, and so it was possible for a child growing up in the 1980s to watch the same animation its parents grew up with in 1960s.

This newly developed animation canon was reflected by the breakthrough film of the 1980s, *Who Framed Roger Rabbit?* The

The Economics of Animation

Because animation is such a high-cost, labour-intensive craft, it has always been closely linked to the economic circumstances of the time. Whereas a great song might be written by anyone, at any time, for no money, great animation cannot be produced without a fair number of talented people and a large amount of time.

Sometimes the economic situation has worked in favour of animation. One of the reasons Disney was able to make the huge strides he did was that the depression of the early 1930s led to huge numbers of commercial artists being out of work. He was able to recruit the best and train them in animation, allowing his studio to develop its classic style. But more often than not, it works against animation, as

happened in the 1970s, when great animators were working on indifferent animation for lack of sufficient funds to finance the kind of animation seen in the Golden Age. Most frequently of all, animation and the economic situation work in an uneasy partnership, where new animation develops alongside technology and methods to make the producing of it cheaper.

UPA Films are a good example of how this happens: founded in 1944, UPA used flat, graphical backgrounds and a stylized form of animation which was radically different from anything done before. Although this was mainly for artistic reasons, other animation companies soon realized that it was a good way of saving on costs, and a range of UPA-style television series were soon appearing.

film was set in the Golden Age and combined animation with live action. Richard Williams directed the animation, which combined the classic hallmarks of the great *Looney Tunes* and Tex Avery films – physical gags, frantic action – with a shadowy, three-dimensional look which would mix well with the film noir feel of the live action. Just as important as the animation was the script, which was very adult-friendly, despite the film being ostensibly aimed at children. The combination of a new, grown up style of script with three-dimensional animation was a taste of what was to come.

The Age of Computers

In 1986 Pixar Films was created and released the short film *Luxo Jnr*. The animation, featuring a small anglepoise lamp jumping round like an excitable puppy, was made entirely with computerized, three-dimensional models. Although this had been done before, previous computer-animated films had been made by the engineers involved in making the software and so lacked the sense of fun and timing which is essential for good animation. The Pixar founder John Lasseter was a trained animator who had previously worked for Disney and thus was able to give his film a real sense of life.

In 1995 Pixar released *Toy Story*, the first ever fully-computer animated feature film. *Toy Story* had a sharp, three-dimensional look which had never been seen before; equally importantly, it had a script which was aimed at adults as well as children. *Toy Story*, and subsequent Pixar films *Toy Story 2*, *Monsters Inc.* and *Finding Nemo*, transformed audiences' perception of what animated films could do, showing filmmakers that there was an alternative to the Disney way of making films. Films such as

Antz and *Shrek* borrowed heavily from Pixar's less cutesy and more knowing style.

However, if computerized animation had a big impact on feature films, it had an even bigger one on the world of drawn animation. With the development of programs making it possible to digitally colour and composite drawings, the traditions of cel animation disappeared almost overnight. Cels were the clear plastic sheets which animation was painted on to once drawn, allowing the background and other layers to be seen behind it. The appearance of computers made cels, and cel painters, redundant. Equally significantly, it took the camera out of animation since drawings were now being rendered by computers rather than captured on film. If these changes were not enough, there were soon programs which would allow you to draw all your animation into a computer from scratch by using a drawing tablet, meaning that it was now possible to do drawn animation without even using a pencil.

ANIMATION TODAY

There are now more different ways of making an animated film than ever before. Computer technology means that it is also cheaper than ever to produce such a film. Programs such as Flash or Toon Boom give you everything you need to make a fully animated, full colour film for relatively little money. Even ten years ago this would have involved cameras, cels, paints and a much bigger budget.

The medium of animation has also grown up since its creation. Although most animation is still aimed at children, the subject matter of cartoons is now more extensive than ever before. As an example of this look at the difference between the non-threatening, family-friendly worlds portrayed in

Animation Around the World

The history of animation may seem to be dominated by films from the English-speaking world. This is far from the case; for almost the whole of its lifespan animation has been produced across the world, often in quite different ways to those familiar to American and British audiences. Even Disney, for many people the epitome of Americanized animation, did much to get animation going in South America by focusing its productions on the area when the war began in Europe.

Apart from Disney, one of the biggest animation studios in the world now is Studio Ghibli, the Japanese company most famous for the Oscar-winning film *Spirited Away*. Although this was the first of their films to prove successful in the English-speaking world, Studio Ghibli, led by the director Hayao Miyasaki, have been making features since the 1980s, including *My Neighbour Totoro* and *Princess Mononoke*. The thoughtful yet child-like view of the world shown in Miyasaki's films is markedly different from the form of animation most readily associated with Japan, that based on the science fiction of *manga* comics such as *Akira* (*manga* is the name given to all comic books, although it is often used to refer particularly to the brand of violent sci-fi of which *Akira* is so typical; animations of *manga* comics are called *anime*). Japanese culture had a high degree of censorship until the 1980s, which *manga* always managed to avoid, and even today *manga* and *anime* are used to show and comment on aspects of Japanese society which might otherwise remain taboo.

Censorship also played a crucial role in the work of the great Czech stop-motion animator Jan Svankmajer. His film *Leonardo's Diary* met with stern disapproval from the Communist government of the time because of its portrayal of the conditions of everyday Czech life. He was consequently banned from making films for seven years and after that restricted to adapting literary classics. This led to him producing the feature film *Alice* in 1987, an animated version of *Alice's Adventures in Wonderland*.

Elsewhere in the world more benevolent government intervention had positive results. The National Film Board of Canada was a government agency set up in 1939 to use film to help people across the world to 'see Canada and see it whole: its people and its purpose'. These grandiose aims saw Canada produce some wonderful and distinctive animation which looked entirely different from that being produced in the United States at the time. *The Cat Came Back*, by Cordell Barker, and Richard Condie's *The Big Snitt* are great examples of the surreal humour of some Canadian animation. Both films were nominated for Oscars, as was *The Street* by Caroline Leaf, which used inks and watercolours to produce stop-motion animation.

Recent years have shown that there is a huge audience for good animation, regardless of the language it is made in. Not only *Spirited Away*, but also the French film *Belleville Rendezvous* (released in the USA as *The Triplets of Belleville*) were hugely successful in 2003. It is to be hoped that their success has encouraged both film distributors and audiences to take a chance on non-English animation.

series such as *The Flintstones* or *Yogi Bear* and compare them with the tone of more recent series such as *The Simpsons* and *South Park.*

There has never been a better time to make an animated film. With the help of this book, and, more importantly, good ideas and an awful lot of hard work, you too can become a small part of animation history.

2 TYPES OF ANIMATION

The aim of this chapter is to go through all the different ways there are of doing animation. In doing so, it will explain the equipment you need, some useful techniques and the advantages and disadvantages associated with each method.

If you are not sure what form of animation to use for your film, then this chapter should answer your questions. Even if you think that you know the kind of animation to use, it is still worth reading about the pros and cons to find out about what is involved. It is best to start with the form of animation that got everything started – drawn animation.

DRAWN ANIMATION

Drawn animation is the original form of animation, as begun by Windsor McCay and famously developed by Disney. In drawn animation movement is created by doing a new drawing for every single frame of the move. To animate someone putting a bottle

This action is animated with five drawings.

down on a table, you would need to draw something like the illustration on page 15.

All the classic animated films – *Snow White*, *Fantasia*, *The Jungle Book* – were produced by using drawn animation. The same may be said of many of the classic cartoon series – *Tom and Jerry*, *Bugs Bunny*, *The Flintstones* and *The Simpsons*.

Equipment

Animation Paper and a Peg Bar The peg bar is taped to the desk or the light box you are working on. Animation paper has three holes punched in it which match up with the three prongs on a peg bar. This ensures that all your drawings are aligned with each other. Peg bars and animation paper can be

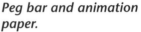

Equipment Needed for Drawn Animation

Drawing
- animation paper
- peg bar
- light box
- pencils
- dope sheet (see below)
- any other specialist drawing or colouring materials your project requires.

Filming
- camera or scanner
- computer

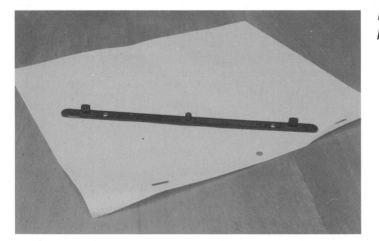

Peg bar and animation paper.

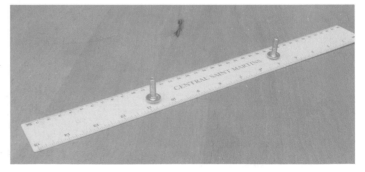

A home-made peg bar.

16

bought only from specialist animation outlets, and the paper can be quite expensive. It is possible to save money by using standard hole-punched paper and making your own peg bar by attaching bolts to a ruler.

A Light Box A light box helps you to animate by letting you see more than one drawing at a time, by shining a light underneath the animation paper. Light boxes can usually be bought from big art shops as well as animation specialists, but they may be expensive too. You can build your own box from fairly simple materials; all you really

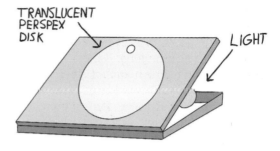

An animation light box.

need is a piece of perspex or glass and a way of propping it up and of shining a light through it.

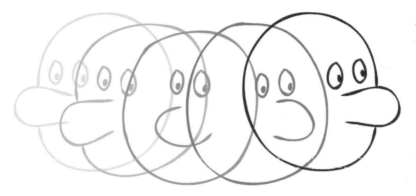

A light box lets you see several drawings at the same time.

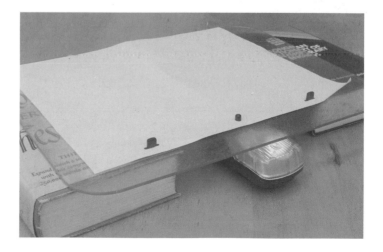

A simple, home-made light box.

Pencils Professional animators tend to use Colerase pencils for their rough drawings, and a clicker pencil for their finished or cleaned up drawings. Colerase pencils give a coloured line which makes it easy to tell the rough drawings from the cleaned up ones at first sight; they also produce a rough, soft line which is easy to rub out.

Clicker pencils are available from most art or office shops, but Colerase can normally be bought only from specialist animation outlets. However, any pencil which is easy to draw with and easy to rub out will be adequate for rough drawings.

Camera When using a camera to capture your drawings, you should try to use the best one that you can get your hands on. Professional animators use digital cameras, as they provide good quality and make it easy to import the final animation into a computer video-editing package. However, it is possible to use a video camera and still

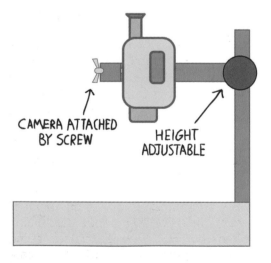

A camera stand will hold your camera in position above your animation.

be able to import the captured animation into a computer by using an analogue-to-digital conversion device. Of course, before the advent of video and digital cameras all animation was shot on film. Doing this has its advantages, not least in that it will give your animation a classic look, but film is an unforgiving medium. With video or digital images you can erase or delete any mistakes, something which is not possible with film; this, along with the fact that much film equipment is available only second-hand, may make it a difficult option.

But whatever camera you eventually use, the most important thing is to make sure that it stays still. If your camera wobbles then your animation will too. Your camera should be firmly attached to a camera stand which allows you to place drawings beneath it.

Once you have your camera in place, you can either connect it up to a computer or opt to use it alone. It is best to use a computer if possible since it allows you to keep working with your drawings after they have been captured. However, if you do not have access to a computer or you are in a hurry, you can use any video camera able to capture images a frame at a time, and then transfer your animation straight to VHS from the camera.

Line-testers Computer programs which capture images for animation are called line-testers. The original line-testing software was called Take Two and worked on Amiga computers. It is still possible to track down second-hand Amigas and they can be a cheap alternative to PC line-testing software. If you are doing this, you will need an Amiga 1200 with 8MBs of extra memory and a hard drive. You will also need a VidiAmiga 12, which will allow you to plug your camera into the Amiga. If you are using a more modern computer, you could try using one of these:

Digicel flip book (www.digicelinc.com) This is often used in animation studios which have moved on from Amigas. It currently only works for the PC.

Animation Stand (www.linker.com) This works on both Mac and PCs; you can download a free, small screen demonstration version.

Quickchecker (www.retas.com) This works on Macs and PCs and a cheaper student licence is available.

Tapptoons Animation Studio and Tapptoons Line-tester (www.tappsplace. freeserve.co. uk) The Animation Studio allows you to do camera moves and add effects as well as simply line-test. The Line-tester program is available to download free of charge but is available on PC only.

Scanner As with cameras, you should try to use the best-quality scanner you can lay your hands on. It is important to attach a peg bar to your scanner so that all your drawings remain aligned when scanned in. You can use a scanner with all but one of the line-testing programs referred to above; the exception is the Amiga. Professional animation companies use scanners to scan into specially designed colouring and compositing programs, such as Toonz or Animo. However, the cost of this software tends to put it out of the reach of individual animators.

As an alternative to such programs, you can import your scanned material into standard picture editing software, such as Photoshop or Illustrator and then use those programs to colour your animation or to

put effects on to it. You could even import the images into computer animation software such as Flash. When colouring or editing your scanned in images, it is important to bear in mind how you want your finished animation to be viewed on a computer or on video. If you are planning to export your finished animation to video, make sure that you know the image format you will be using. *See* Chapter 9 for further information on showing your film.

Advantages of Drawn Animation

- It is the best form of animation for capturing realistic human movement. It is very hard to do lifelike drawing straight into a computer, and equally difficult to construct lifelike models for 3D or stop-motion animation. If you are animating any reasonably realistic character dancing, playing sport or having a sword fight drawn animation is the best medium to use.

- Drawn animation opens up a huge range of stylistic possibilities; not everything has to look like Disney. You can use thick, wobbly lines and simple characters like Bob Godfrey (famous in Britain for the children's series *Henry's Cat* and *Roobarb and Custard*, and also an Oscar winner) or flowing ink lines like Michael Dudok de Wit, (another Oscar winner for his film *Father and Daughter*). With styles like this, characters and objects can wobble or flow with a life of their own, something which is hard to do with other forms of animation.

- Using drawn animation gives you complete control over every single frame of your film; 2D or 3D computer animation often (but not always) involves letting the computer automatically create frames in between two key points, which may give the resulting animation an arti-

Using Dope Sheets: Timing for Non-computer Animation

Animation is all about keeping control over very small amounts of time; one frame is only 0.04sec long. In computer animation you have a time-line which automatically keeps track of the images in each frame. However, if you are doing drawn or model animation you need to keep track of time by using something called a dope sheet. A dope sheet (the name originated, like animation itself, from the USA in the 1920s where 'dope' meant knowledge) allows you to keep track of what is in each frame on each layer of your animation. It also lets you record other information about your animation.

Dope sheets should be used from the moment you start animating. For instance, once you have drawn your key positions and used a line-tester to work out the timings, you should write them into your dope sheet. This will help you when drawing your in-betweens, since by glancing at your dope sheet you will see how many in-betweens are needed. Opposite you can see how a simple piece of animation would look when shown on a dope sheet.

Production				Levels			Scene
Sound	Action	Frame Numbers	Top			Bottom	Camera
		1					
		2					
		3					
		4					
		5					
THIS COLUMN	USE THIS	6					CAMERA MOVES
CAN BE USED	COLUMN TO	7	←		→		CAN BE WRITTEN
TO SHOW	WRITE NOTES	8	USE THIS SPACE TO SHOW THE				HERE.
WHEN SOUND	SHOWING	9	FRAME AND LEVEL AN IMAGE				
EFFECTS AND	WHAT ACTION	10	GOES IN.				
LIP-SYNCH	HAPPENS						
OCCUR.	WHEN						

A dope sheet can record every piece of information about your film.

This animation has three layers: one for the character, one for the anvil and one for the background.

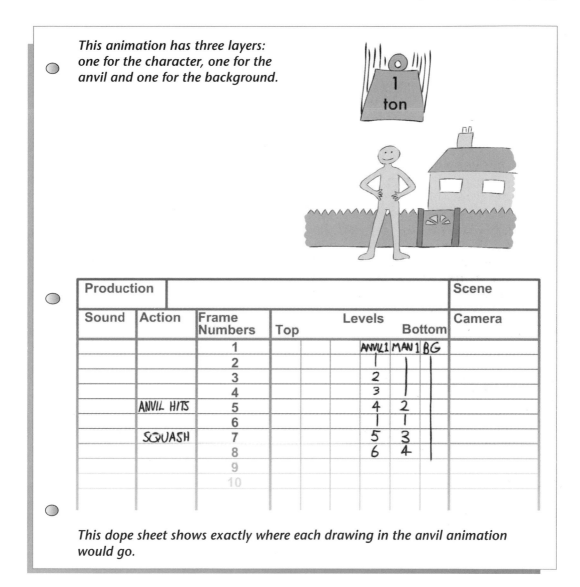

Production				Scene	
Sound	**Action**	**Frame Numbers**	**Top** — Levels — **Bottom**		**Camera**
		1		ANVL1 MAN1 BG	
		2			
		3	2		
		4	3		
	ANVIL HITS	5	4	2	
		6			
	SQUASH	7	5	3	
		8	6	4	
		9			
		10			

This dope sheet shows exactly where each drawing in the anvil animation would go.

ficial, floaty feel. With drawn animation, you create every single frame.

Disadvantages of Drawn Animation

Drawn animation is very time-consuming to prepare. You can save time and work by using the techniques known as 'limited animation' (*see* Chapter 7), but for realistic cinematic animation, you will need at least twelve drawings for each second of animation.

All these drawings will need to be coloured, which is even more time-consuming. It is worth bearing in mind that professional drawn animation projects can often spend almost half of their budgets on colouring.

In drawn animation you need to work very hard to keep your characters looking the same throughout the film. This is called keeping your characters 'on model', and is dealt with by using model sheets (*see* Chapter 4).

Useful Techniques in Drawn Animation

Use layers wherever possible Redrawing every single element of your scene every time you want something to happen is very time-consuming. As an additional problem, however hard you try to trace an object accurately, you will always be slightly imprecise; this will cause the line you have traced to appear to wobble when you play your animation. To avoid these problems, animators separate out distinct parts of their scene into different layers. For example, if you were animating two characters talking in front of a shop, the shop would stay the same in every drawing. However, if you did all your animation on one layer, then, every time one of your characters moved, you would have to redraw the entire shop. To avoid this, you could draw your shop on a separate layer and then place the two characters on top of it.

If your two characters moved at different times you could put these characters on separate layers too. When putting together your final animation you can use a computer to put the layers on top of each other and make the blank areas transparent. The accompanying illustration shows how this works. Before computers were used in animation, this process was done on camera by tracing drawings on to transparent cels which were then layered on top of each other in the same way.

There were exceptions to this process of layering; Bob Godfrey, the Oscar-winning animator behind the 1970s series *Roobarb*

This is how three different layers can be put together to make a scene. The use of layers saves the redrawing of all the elements in the scene every time one of them moves.

and *Custard*, would often do all his animation straight on to paper. As he had no transparent cel to put a background behind, the background would be redrawn for every single frame. This process inevitably meant the background would change slightly from drawing to drawing, and the animators on *Roobarb and Custard* would deliberately exaggerate this, doing intentionally inaccurate tracings to give everything a distinctively wobbly look.

Test your key drawings before animating
Because drawn animation is so time-consuming it is best to be as sure as you can that something will work before you begin to do all the drawings required. To do this, shoot your key drawings before drawing any in-betweens. Once your key drawings are in a line-testing program, or any program with a timeline, you can space them out over time and watch them. Even though you do not have all the drawings, you should still be able to tell whether your animation is working. Doing this allows you to play with different timings without having to do all the drawings. Only start to do

the drawings when you are happy with the timing. See the accompanying box on key animation and straightahead to find out how key drawings work.

Do not try to animate everything at once
Having spent some time in designing a character, it is often tempting to begin your animation by drawing every element of it in every drawing. However, this may make matters confusing. If you were animating the character shown below you would have to concentrate on getting the basic movement of the animation right as well as drawing all the details of his costume. As well as being confusing, this would mean spending a fair amount of time on each drawing. Much of this could be wasted if, on line-testing, it turns out that your character positions do not work.

To save on time and to make your job of animating easier, it is better to animate one thing at a time. With this character you could begin by doing key drawings, using just an outline of the body shape; you could then add the details of the dog and costume to the keys; and finally, having done

Save time by animating one thing at a time and building up to the final character. Start with the basic body elements, add the details and leave any follow-through animation until the last, and animate it straightahead.

23

Key Animation vs. Straightahead

Key animation and straightahead animation are the two ways of animating a move. When animating straightahead you begin with the first drawing then do the second, the third and so on.

In key animation the important or key drawings of a move are drawn first. The drawings in between these keys (literally called 'in-betweens') are only drawn once the keys are finished to satisfaction. The drawings below show a man kicking a football, animated straightahead and with keys.

Animators use key and straightahead animation to create different effects. Key animation is best used when animating characters or anything which is moving in a controlled way. This is because keys allow you to plan all the important parts of a move and to keep everything organized and under control. Straightahead animation is used to animate anything which moves in a spontaneous or flowing way, water, for example, or a flag rippling in the breeze. It is ideal for what is called 'follow-through animation', a flapping tail or a cloak trailing behind a character. Animating these using key animation tends not to work; it gives the impression that the water you are animating is being controlled and loses the flowing sense that such animation needs.

It is often possible to use key and straightahead animation within the same move. For instance, when animating a footballer it would be best to use key animation for the main body movement and straightahead animation for his long, flowing hair.

This move was animated by doing all of the drawings in order: straightahead animation.

This move was animated using key drawings.

Equipment Needed for 3D Animation

For 3D animation you simply need a computer and one of a number of 3D animation packages. 3D animation is a complex operation and as such requires a fairly powerful computer. The major 3D animation packages and the minimum system requirements are listed below.

Maya	Windows XP Professional, 2000 Professional (Service Pack 2 or higher)
	Mac OS 9, OS X 10.1 OS X 10.2
Softimage	Windows XP Pro, 2000
	Linux
3D Studio Max	Windows 2000, NT 4

Always check the specific system requirements of any package you are buying. As a general rule, at the very least you will need a computer with:

* Intel Pentium II or higher or an AMD Athlon processor
* 512MB RAM
* Hardware-Accelerated OpenGL graphics card
* 450MB of hard disk space

the in-betweens, draw the flowing cape and trailing ears using straightahead animation.

3D ANIMATION

3D animation is a form of computer animation which uses three-dimensional models built within a computer. Rather than re-drawing the characters in every frame, 3D animation involves moving character models around, much as is done in model animation (*see* below).

3D animation was made famous by Pixar, the company responsible for, most recently, *Finding Nemo*. It is also being used more and more in television series, as well as in computer games.

It is worth noting that all the 3D packages are designed for operating systems rarely used on home computers (for instance, home PCs come with Windows ME

instead of 2000). These packages are expensive, costing thousands, rather than hundreds of pounds.

Maya produce a personal learning edition which you can download for free. Although this is useful for practising animation, it cannot be used to produce an animated film because the software places a watermark text image over all rendered images.

Softimage produce an educational version which costs a fraction of the full price; however, as with the Maya learning edition, this cannot be used to produce finished films.

Advantages of 3D Animation
* The use of a computer means that you no longer have to produce an image for every single frame. It is possible to set up key positions and then let the computer automatically produce the in-between

images. By carefully controlling the way the computer creates these in-betweens, it is possible to save much time on animation.

- A film made with 3D animation will have a very particular, modern look. The majority of the successful animated films made in the last five years have been done in 3D. If you are aiming to emulate the films made by Pixar, as well as other films such as *Shrek*, then you will need to use 3D animation.

- 3D animation makes the hard things easy. Animating a complicated camera move where the camera spins round a character would take a long time in drawn animation and would also be laborious to set up using models and a real camera. 3D animating software will let you move the computerized camera in an instant.

Disadvantages of 3D Animation

- As well as making the hard things easy, 3D animation may make the easy things hard, especially for the beginner. You may find yourself having to deal with a range of problems – characters walking through the floor, floating through the air or moving their arms through their own bodies – which would not exist in other forms of animation.

- To do 3D animation well is a very expensive process and there are no real short cuts to avoid this expense. A further problem is that whereas cheap, limited forms of other animation may still look quite stylish, cheap 3D animation tends to just look unfinished. Cheaply made, drawn television series (*Dangermouse*), or cheaply made, cut out animation series (*South Park*, *Pugwash*) can still have a memorable look and style. At the moment, the software and man-hours

required mean this is rarely the case with 3D animation.

- Many find it harder to create animation with real character in 3D. It is perfectly possible, as the Pixar films show, but, equally, many find it easier to draw a convincing character on paper or construct it out of plasticine than to model it in a computer.

Useful Techniques in 3D Animation

Do not let the computer do too much animation It may be tempting to set up the bare minimum of key positions and then let most of your animation be done by the computer's automated in-betweens. However, doing this will make your animation seem floaty and weightless. Although it is possible to do good animation by using automated in-betweens, you need to use them in the right place. You also need to make very good use of the function curves which allow you to control the in-betweens.

If you find yourself continually tweaking an in-between to get it working, it probably means that you need to do more key animation. Do not let the computer turn you into a lazy animator.

Cheat wherever possible Do not worry about your animation being anatomically perfect from every single angle; after all, your audience are going to see it from only the one angle. Good 3D animators often cheat with their models, moving arms out of place or through other parts of the body out of sight of the camera to get a better pose.

On the subject of camera positions, do not be tempted to show your animation from a ridiculous angle just because you can. All animation benefits from being shown from an angle giving you a clear,

This pose is easy to understand from this camera angle ...

... but an unusual camera angle makes the same pose much less clear.

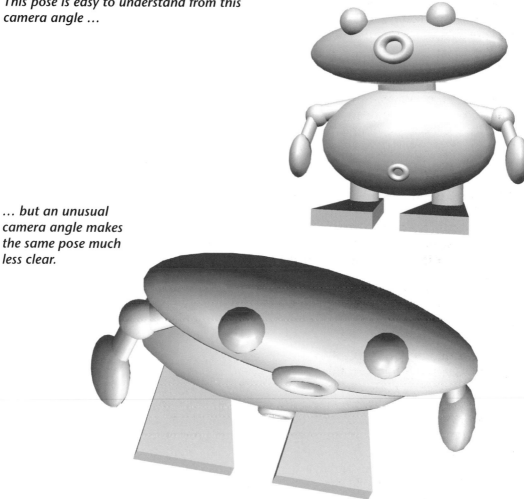

silhouetted profile of what is happening, and 3D animation is no different.

Choose your speciality 3D software lets you do all manner of things as well as animate: you can texture your characters, light scenes, model characters and backgrounds, and combine animation with live action. Few, if any, try to master all these skills; most 3D animators never work with the modelling or texturing tools, they just ani-

mate. It is best to concentrate on the areas of 3D animation which appeal to you and which you are good at.

2D COMPUTER ANIMATION

2D computer animation is not a separate form of an animation, but rather a way of combining the techniques of drawn and cut-out animation and using a computer to do them more quickly.

When doing drawn animation straight into a computer, you can save time by copying and pasting animation you want to reuse, enlarging it or flipping it as you do so. When doing cut-out, you can organize the different pieces of your puppet into a structured character library, which makes it easy to select the pieces you need to animate. You also have the option of setting up keys and getting the computer to do automated in-betweens (although, as with 3D animation, you need to think carefully about how you do this to avoid your animation's losing its sense of life). This is a fairly new way of animating and is mostly used for television series; *2DTV* and *Monkeydust* were both animated in this way.

2D Animation Programs

There are a number of animation programs you can use to do 2D computer animation:

Flash Probably the most widely used program. It was actually designed for web design and online animation. However, animators soon realized that it was a cheap way of animating and colouring animation for television. Flash is highly flexible,

---

Equipment Needed for 2D Computer Animation

- computer
- 2D animation program
- drawing tablet (optional)

Computer As with 3D animation, you should try to use the best computer you can get your hands on.

System requirements

Flash	Windows XP, 2000, 98, ME
	Linux RedHat 7.3 or 8.0
	Mac OS X 10.2.4 or higher (Maya Complete only)
Moho	Windows 95, 98, ME, NT4, 2000, XP
	Mac OS X
	Linux Red Hat 8.0, SuSE 8.2, Mandrake 9.0, 9.1, Gentoo, Debian SID, Knoppix
Toon Boom Studio	Windows XP, 2000, 98, ME
	Mac OS X

Always check the specific system requirements of any package you are buying. At the very least, what you will need to do 2D computer animation is:

- Intel Pentium II or higher processor or equivalent
- Windows 98 SE (4.10.2222 A), Windows 2000 or Windows XP
- 128MB RAM
- 275 MB available disk space

---

but as it was not designed with animators in mind it can be difficult for those with a background in drawn animation to get used to.

Toon Boom Studio This program was designed specifically for animators, and its interface aims to mirror the set up of drawn animation as much as possible. However, compared with Flash it has fewer options for exporting finished animation, which means that it may be tricky to use in conjunction with other programs such as Flash or After FX. You can get round this problem by buying a plug-in which will allow you to import Toon Boom projects into Flash.

Moho This is a new 2D animation program which differs from Toon Boom and Flash in two important ways. Firstly, it was designed with the aim that you do all your animation inside the program and so there is no option to scan in drawings. Secondly, it allows you to build a skeleton for your puppets, so that all the pieces of your cut-out style character are connected and move together. This is a similar system to that used in Celaction, the package used to make series such as *The Big Knights* and *2DTV*; however, Celaction is currently made available only to animation companies and not to individual animators.

It is worth noting that, unlike 3D packages, all these programs are designed to run on the kind of operating system you will find on home computers. They are also much cheaper than 3D packages.

Drawing Tablet

Often called Wacom tablets after the most well-known brand, these will allow you to draw straight into your animation program by using a special pen on a pressure-sensi-tive pad connected to the computer. Although they take a little getting used to, using a drawing tablet will be much easier than attempting to draw with a mouse.

Advantages of 2D Computer Animation

- It is the quickest way of producing full-colour, finished animation at home. Whereas drawn animation needs to go through a separate colouring process after it has been animated, and 3D animation has to be textured and lighted, 2D animation can be finished much more quickly. This is worth considering if you are short of time, money or help when making your film.
- The ability to copy and paste animation or to make slight adjustments to an existing piece of animation to reuse it in a different situation is hugely useful. It is at its most beneficial where you are using the same character again and again since this will give you more opportunities to reuse your work. This is why 2D computer animation is widely used in television series, where the same characters appear in every episode.

Disadvantages of 2D Computer Animation:

- Although a drawing tablet is a vast improvement on drawing with a mouse, if you are doing any form of flowing or highly realistic movement, then it is still much easier to draw on paper.
- Although using a computer can help your animation, it may also mean that it loses the quirky personal touches that give it life. A scribbly drawing or a hand-made plasticine model will often have an innate sense of character which can be harder to communicate by using a computer.

Techniques for 2D Computer Animation

In the main, the skills required to do good computer animation are the same as those needed for drawn and cutout animation, described elsewhere in this chapter. One other thing to remember is to use your automated in-betweens with great care. Flash, in particular, makes it easy to move characters and elements across the screen automatically, but this often makes your animation look robotic and lifeless.

Automated in-betweens may be used to good effect, such as scrolling a background or moving some individual body parts of a character, but it is important to avoid using them for everything.

STOP-MOTION ANIMATION

Stop-motion animation covers all styles of animation which are done by using straight-ahead animation in front of a camera. Whereas in drawn or computer animation

This mouse was moved a frame at a time to create animation.

you create key positions which you can experiment with before animating, in stop-motion you move your animation a frame at a time, capturing each frame in front of the camera as you go along. This form of animation is used because it allows you to work with materials which cannot be used in conventional keyed animation. This can mean anything from animating by using old teddy bears or other toys, to creating an oil painting on glass and moving the paint around every frame to create movement.

As you can see, stop-motion animation can be done with any image or substance

It is possible to animate by manipulating paint on glass.

which can be moved around in front of a camera. It is worth looking at the films of the Czech animator Jan Svankmajer to see the potential of stop-motion. Rather than go through every possible version of stop-motion animation, we shall concentrate on the two most widely used forms: cut-out and model animation.

CUT-OUT ANIMATION

Cut-out animation is a form of stop-motion animation. Although it makes use of drawings, it is different from drawn animation because, instead of drawing every frame, you draw a character model which is cut out and turned into a two-dimensional puppet. You then animate this puppet straightahead into a camera (*see* above for notes on key animation versus straight-ahead on page 24).

A famous example of cut-out animation is *South Park*, one of the most successful and most basically animated series of all time.

Equipment Needed for Cut-out Animation

paper
pencils
camera
dope sheet (*see* 'Drawn Animation')
computer and line-testing software (*see* 'Drawn Animation').

Camera
You will need a camera that will allow you to capture images a frame at a time and to view them instantly. Digital video cameras have become much cheaper and one of these rigged up to a PC with line-testing software will allow you do cut-out animation. As with any line-tester, it is vital to keep the camera rigid (*see* 'Drawn Animation' for more details).

Depending on how you want your finished film to be viewed, it would be possible to shoot it on camera and transfer it straight to video. However, if you want some control over your captured images it is better to use a line-tester.

A character animated in drawn animation might look like this.

But to represent such a character in cut-out animation you would draw all the pieces of a puppet ...

... and then put them together under the camera to animate.

Another notable example is Terry Gilliam's animation in the *Monty Python* films and series. Cut-out animation was also used to make the classic children's television series *Captain Pugwash* and *Pigeon Street*.

Advantages of Cut-out Animation
- Cut-out animation is a very quick way of getting something animated. If you have a good idea for your film but not very much time nor money to make it, then simple, stylized cut-out animation will take you a long way – just look at *South Park.*
- Cut-out animation allows you to make use of much more detailed character drawings than you could use in other forms of animation. Because you are drawing a character only once, your drawing may be much more intricate. Terry Gilliam is the perfect example of this; he would often use characters based on medieval Bible illustrations or Renaissance painting, which would be hugely complex and time-consuming to animate using drawn animation.
- Cut-out animation always has a fairly unusual look to it; the use of two-dimensional puppets means that you often need to use a huge level of artistic licence to move your characters around successfully. A good example of this is the classic series *Mr Ben* in which the title character had a walk cycle which, although totally

32

unrealistic, was very funny and memorable. Cut-out animation almost always has some element of this quirky, odd, but entertaining movement.

Disadvantages of Cut out Animation

- The unique sense of movement you get from using cut-out puppets will not suit everybody nor every idea. If you want to show realistic or flowing movement, then cut-out animation is not the best medium to use.
- There is no way of using keys in cut-out animation; you have to shoot it all straightahead. It is possible to shoot the key positions of your move to gain an idea of the timing you want to work to, but you will ultimately have to shoot it by moving your puppet along, bit by bit,

frame after frame. If you want to have a cut-out style with the option of using keys, you need to think about using 2D computer animation (*see* above).

Useful Techniques in Cut-out Animation

Plan out your animation carefully before shooting It is easy to be carried away when doing straightahead animation and lose track of timing. It is always worth working out the time you want any move to take before you start animating. This avoids your having to reshoot a move which is too slow or too fast.

Think carefully about how your character is going to move before designing your puppet It is best to think about the kind of movement your character will do before

This cut-out puppet has separate eyebrows to allow a range of expressions.

Three head positions for a cut-out puppet.

you animate it. This will prevent your having to redesign a puppet halfway through your animation, which could cause your character's appearance to change. Any part of your character which you want to be able to move independently needs to be a separate part of the puppet. For example, if you want your character to be able to move his eyebrows then they need to be separate from the head.

Make a puppet which gives you options
It is possible to do several drawings for the same body part – these may then be swapped as required. For example, the puppet at the bottom of page 33 has three different head positions, all of which may be fitted on to the same body.

MODEL ANIMATION

Model animation is a form of stop-motion animation, done with real (not computer-generated) three-dimensional models. As with other forms of stop-motion animation, you have to animate straightahead.

The most famous model animation in the world is done by Aardman Animation, the company which won Oscars for the *Wallace and Gromit* films, and also went on to make *Chicken Run*. Before Aardman, the most famous model animation series was probably *The Magic Roundabout*.

Model-making Equipment
With model-making equipment much depends on the size and detail of the character you are making. A lot of model animation is done using plasticine modelling clay. Sometimes this can be used on its own, but for bigger characters it is worth using wire to build a basic skeleton to support the model's weight. It is also worth remembering that plasticine distorts easily, and,

although this is good when it comes to moving your model, it may mean that smaller features such as eyes lose their shape quickly. To avoid this, you could use beads or pins to make eyes and noses.

Of course, you do not have to make your model from plasticine. You can use wood, metal, anything which will let you build a character that moves, and, even more importantly, hold a pose while you film it.

Advantages of Model Animation
- Model characters almost always have a great deal of character about them; there is something about a real, hand-made look that gives them a personality which can be hard to achieve by using computers.
- Model animation is one of the best forms of animation for animating subtle facial expressions. This is because it makes it easy to get the kind of texture and detail which would take a long time to draw or build in a computer.
- Because model characters exist in real space, a wide range of different props and even characters can be made out of everyday objects. In *Morph*, the 1970s television series made by Aardman co-founder Peter Lord, there was a dog which was nothing more than a nail-brush animated to chase around the set in a suitably doggy way. Using real-life objects such as this gives your animation

---

○ **Equipment Needed for Model Animation**

camera
line-tester (*see* page 18)
○ model-making equipment

With simple materials you can produce a character for model animation.

a very different look, not to mention saving time on character design.

Disadvantages of Model Animation

Model animation is one of the least forgiving forms of animation to use – once you have moved a character on from a position it is difficult if not impossible to get that exact position back. This means that, if something goes wrong with your move, more often than not you just have to start again.

Scenes with many characters in them can be awkward to do in model animation. You have to move each character before capturing the image and this may be tricky for two reasons. First, it can be hard to concentrate on four characters' movements at one time, remembering exactly what stage each body part of each character is in the move. Secondly, if your characters are close together it may be hard to move one of them without knocking all the others over.

USEFUL TECHNIQUES IN MODEL ANIMATION

As with all stop-motion animation, you need to plan out your character moves carefully in advance, as it will be impossible to change them once they have been animated.

One thing worth bearing in mind when building your models for animation is how they will deteriorate during filming. If you are using a plasticine model you will find that, after using it for a while, parts will start to look rather tattered. You can get around this problem by having a production line of body parts – when you are modelling your character, make several versions of each part, rather than just one. This will allow you to keep all your character parts looking precisely the same as each other, or 'on model'. If you do not do this you will run the risk of your character's appearance changing throughout the film, as new parts made at different times are introduced.

3   IDEAS AND PLANNING

In this chapter we shall be looking at the creative and practical work involved in getting your film started. People sometimes make the mistake of seeing animation as a purely creative medium. Although there is a huge amount of creativity involved in animation, an animated film cannot be made without a great deal of organization and planning. A dramatic, spontaneous painting can be created by a single artist in one inspired bout of creativity. An equally dramatic and as apparently spontaneous piece of animation will need a small team of people working on it for weeks, possibly months. Animation is such a labour-intensive craft that you cannot afford to leave things to chance. You need to be sure about what you want a scene to look like, how long it will last and how it links to the scenes before and after it *before* you start animating it, not after. A tricky scene could easily take a week to animate, which is time you cannot afford to waste.

But before we look at some ways of planning your film we shall look at the creative side of the process and how you can use it to make the practical side of things as easy as possible.

IDEAS

It could be argued that ideas are the one thing this book cannot, and indeed should not, attempt to teach on the grounds that a good idea can come only from an individual's imagination and that there should be no limit placed on this imagination. While the first part of this argument is clearly true, the second part of it – that imagination exists outside any practical limitations – certainly is not.

A look at the highly imaginative films made by Pixar is enough to confirm that even Hollywood filmmakers have to keep their ideas practical. When Pixar came to make their first feature film, they knew that their human 3D characters looked far from believable. The company had yet to work out a way of successfully animating hair, and this, combined with the puppet-style of animation used, made the characters look a little wooden. Rather than ignoring these problems, Pixar used them to shape their ideas. The result was *Toy Story*, a beautifully animated film starring toys made of wood and plastic. The idea fully matched the animation.

Pixar are a perfect example of how the practical limitations involved in animation can actually stimulate your ideas instead of restricting them. As the limitations changed, the studio found that new ideas became possible. Once they had developed a system for animating hair and fur they were able to make *Monsters Inc.*, with the very hairy Sully as a lead character.

Having Ideas that Work
Most people have at some point started something which seemed like a good idea

Changing the layout of this scene makes it much easier to animate.

at the time but turned out to be impossible to complete. When it comes to an idea for an animated film you should look at three key areas to avoid this happening.

Fitting your ideas to your animation
Much as Pixar did with *Toy Story*, you need to think how your idea matches up to the animation you will be using. If you already know what kind of animation you are going to use for your film, then you need to look at its limitations and see how they will affect your ideas. Conversely, if you are fairly sure of your idea but uncertain how to do it, you will need to think about how your idea would work with different kinds of animation. *See* Chapter 2 for more on the advantages and disadvantages of different types of animation.

As well as considering the style of animation you will be using, it is equally important to bear in mind the abilities of the people animating your film. If you or the people working with you have little animation experience then it would be unwise to an attempt a twenty-first century reworking of *Fantasia*. It is important to keep your idea within reach of your animators' abilities and not to end by making a film featuring a series of wildly ambitious but unsuccessfully animated ideas. This does not mean that you have to abandon animating anything complicated, but that you need to put

some thought into how you animate it. For example, although four-legged walk cycles are notoriously tricky to animate, it can still be relatively easy to make a film featuring dogs, horses or any other four-legged beast you choose. All that is needed is a careful consideration of how you animate your animals; use close-ups or obscure their legs with hedges or fences, anything to avoid getting bogged down in a walk cycle that you feel may be beyond you.

Take a look at any film featuring four-legged animals and you will be amazed at the tricks used to avoid animating too many four-legged walk or run cycles. *See* Chapter 7 for more on the art of limited animation.

Fitting your ideas to your budget Having an idea which works within your budget is very important; if you get it wrong, you will find yourself reaching the end of the time and money set aside for making your film and only be halfway through completing it. If you want to avoid this you need to be realistic about what you can and cannot do. Once again, this does not necessarily mean restricting your ideas, but just thinking about how you go about making them reality.

For example, if you are making a film about dinosaurs you may well be keen on their looking as frighteningly realistic as possible. However, even if you have the 3D animation equipment and know-how to create a realistic looking dinosaur film, it is highly unlikely that you will have the time and money needed to animate it. There are two ways of getting around this problem. The first is to change your original idea. instead of using realistic dinosaurs, stylize your animation so that it is quicker and easier to do. However, if you are reluctant to abandon your dreams of realistic dinosaurs, then you may want to consider an alternative approach: instead of changing your dinosaurs' appearance, you can change the way they are used. Rather than animating a *Tyrannosaurus rex* rampaging towards the camera in full view, you can create an equally dramatic effect by a single, snatched close-up of an eye or a claw or even by showing a silhouette on a cave wall. This technique of hinting at a creature's presence without properly showing it to the audience has been used in cinema for years. The *Jaws* films would indicate the shark by showing a fin on the horizon, or sometimes by just playing that famously scary music. More recently, the first *Jurassic Park* film, which one would think featured realistic dinosaurs in abundance, actually contained only 6½ minutes of dinosaur animation.

Fitting your ideas to the length of your animation This is perhaps less relevant than the issues surrounding the budget and animation, for the simple reason that most animated films are short since there is usually neither the time nor the money to make something lasting half an hour or longer. Having said that, it is worth pointing out that an idea that makes a good 5-minute short film may not make such a good half-hour television show or feature-length movie.

Tom and Jerry is a good example. The idea of a hopeless cat chasing a clever mouse frantically and unsuccessfully around the house is very funny for the 5 or so minutes it normally lasts. Over half an hour or longer, the idea begins to wear thin; there are only so many different objects that Tom can bump into, and the viewers' eyes begin to get worn out by the hectic pace of the animation. When it came to making a feature-length *Tom and Jerry* the original idea had to be tweaked substantially to give it a chance of working over 90 minutes. However, these changes – particularly the one of giving the characters voices – took the film so far away from the original idea that it lost its appeal to fans of the original films.

The Simpsons is another good example of an idea having an ideal length. It only really flourished when it changed from being a short, 5-minute sketch on *The Tracey Ullman Show* into 25-minute long episodes. These longer episodes gave the characters time to develop, allowing for a greater range of jokes and situations than could happen within 5 minutes. Interestingly, the makers of the show have so far shown little interest in producing a feature-length *Simpsons*, suggesting that they are aware of the right time length for their animation.

PLANNING

Having settled on an idea that works and fits with the style and length of your animation, as well as with your budget, you need to start planning how you are going to make that idea actually happen. Planning your film is all about being thorough: going through every aspect of your film and making sure that everything is in place before you start work. Once you have done that, you can start thinking about how the process of filmmaking will work – who will do what and when – and even create a schedule for filming. However, before doing that you will need to identify every single thing that you will need for filming.

What Do You Need?

Equipment This is the easiest area to plan. It should be fairly straightforward to work out what you need, be it a computer, a camera, modelling clay or dope sheets. But to actually get hold of these could be slightly harder: specialist animation equipment (peg bars, animation paper, dope sheets) will need to be ordered, so make sure that you allow time for it all to arrive before you start filming (*see* the list of suppliers to find out more about ordering specialist animation equipment).

It is also important to test your equipment before beginning filming to make sure that it works the way you want it to. For instance, if you are planning to make a 2D computer film, it is worth checking to see whether the computer you are using will be able to play through your finished, animated scenes at full speed. On an average computer scenes with lots of animation and intricate backgrounds will often play through at slower speeds or sometimes not play at all. There are ways around this – leaving the backgrounds off until the last minute or exporting your scenes as avi or QuickTime files to test them – but these will affect how you work.

People Think about all the different jobs which will need to be done to complete your film: voice-overs, backgrounds, animation, special effects, character design; then think about how many of them you are able to do yourself. This requires a certain amount of honesty; it is easy to get carried away and decide that you can do everything yourself, but this is unlikely to be the case. Even if it is just a particular voice you need for a character or some technical help with putting the finished film together, you will almost always need some help.

Once you have identified the areas you need help with, you need to find the right people to help you. When making your own film you are bound to be short of money, so always check whether friends and family will help you for free before you start looking for anyone else. This is particularly the case with voice-overs – professional voice-over artists can be costly, but most people have a friend with a moderate talent for mimicry who can be flattered into voicing a character free of charge.

Once you have exhausted the possibilities of your own social circle it is always worth approaching your local art school to see whether any students studying animation or film-making would be interested in co-operating with you. You will often find people interested in gaining the experience of working on a film and consequently prepared to work for little or no money.

However, you should not expect everyone you ask to work on your film to give his or her help for free. Although you will naturally be excited about your film and prepared to spend as much time as necessary to complete it, others are likely to be prepared to work on it only if they can gain something from it, be it experience or money. It is worth weighing up the advantages and disadvantages of using people prepared to work for little or no money. The obvious advantage is that you will save money and, into the bargain, get bright, enthusiastic and quite possibly very talented people. The often overlooked disadvantage is that it will be almost impossible to hold these people to work deadlines or make them provide work of a certain standard. Once people are working for no money, albeit to gain experience, you will have to accept all the limitations that entails, such as their only being able to work outside college hours or having to give priority to other jobs which are actually paying them. In short, if you have a small but important job on your film which you want done professionally, it is worth considering paying someone to do it.

To find professional help for your film you could consult the specialist media guides listed in the Bibliography. Depending on what you are after, it is often worth looking in your local classified telephone directory under video or audiovisual equipment; you will often find small companies who will be able to put your computer animation on to video or edit your film for much less than a specialized animation company might charge.

Budget As mentioned above, you are likely to be short on money when it comes to making your own film. Because of this, you will need to be careful when planning how much your film will cost – your budget. Most personal animated films start out with a budget of zero, with all the work being provided free by the person whose idea the film is, along with a few friends and relatives. If this is the case with your film, then you can move on to the section on scheduling; planning your time is even more important if you have no money to spare.

However, if you do have some money to spend on your film then you need to work out how far it will go. Even more importantly, if you are trying to obtain funding from a production company interested in your idea or a charity which funds young filmmakers, then you need to know how much money to ask for. It can be hard to work out how much money it will take to make your film when you have never made one before. The following points should help you work out a sensible budget.

Concentrate on the part of the film which will be the most difficult to make since this is usually the most expensive. It is all too easy to end up concentrating on the areas which will be most enjoyable and relegate other, more time-consuming and costly areas of the work to the back of your mind. While it is perfectly reasonable to look forward to the fun parts of filmmaking, there is no point in spending weeks sketching backgrounds, experimenting with paints and trying out different colour schemes if you end up with countless beautiful backgrounds but a script that is only half finished. When you first think of your idea for a film, try to identify those parts of it that will be hardest to do and concentrate on how you will do them, and on how much time and money it will take to do them.

Always assume that things will take longer than they should. It is easy to think of an idea which should, if everything goes well, be animated within, say, six weeks. However, as a rule of thumb, something always goes wrong. Always allow for some contingency money in your budget, set aside about 10 per cent of your budget for use in case of emergencies.

If you are trying to get funding for your film, then you will need to consider how much money you will work for. Although the idea of deciding your own pay sounds attractive at first, it is actually a very taxing thing to do. You need to work out two figures: first, the minimum amount you can afford to live on for the time it will take to make the film, and, secondly, the maximum amount you think people will be prepared to give you. Working out the first figure is fairly straightforward; working out the second involves a certain amount of guesswork. In Britain, the union which represents animators, BECTU, produces a list outlining the minimum pay which can be expected for all the jobs involved in animation.

When seeking funding try to avoid asking for one large sum. Instead, break your budget down into smaller amounts covering separate areas of the film – voice recording, animation and so on. With luck, the person, company or funding agency you are approaching will look at these amounts and then add on some more for contingency. Another tip to bear in mind is to avoid naming a range of money; if you say you need from £4,000 to £6,000 to make your film, you will almost always get £4,000. Be honest about what you need; if your idea cannot be realized without that £6,000, then say so, or be prepared to modify your proposal.

Scheduling Your Film

Scheduling is all about making sure that you do the right things in the right order. Although this sounds straightforward, it is amazing how many people try to do things in the wrong order (and not just beginners, but experienced animators and film-makers as well).

The most common reason for getting things in the wrong order is a desire to begin animating before the script is finished. Countless animators have tried this and it never works. Without a complete script, you can never be sure exactly how your film will turn out. For instance, you may know that you are going to end the film with a heroic sword fight, but do you know exactly how this fight will begin or what plot details you need to get across to the audience to make it clear why your characters are fighting? It is easy to fall into the trap of assuming that these details will sort themselves out, and even to start believing that even thinking about these

details will hamper your creativity. Nothing could be further from the truth; getting the details right is an integral part of the creative process, not an obstacle to be overcome or an irritant to be ignored. This is the case with all kinds of film-making, but it is particularly true of animation. After all, an animated film is made up of nothing but details; the labour spent on a single frame of animation may go unnoticed on its own, but it is the combination of thousands of such detailed frames, all of which have had much work put into them, that makes a film work.

In general, the best order to do things is:

1. script
2. character design
3. background design
4. storyboard
5. lay out
6. voice-recording
7. animation
8. sound effects
9. post-production

To organize your film successfully, work out how long each of these individual elements will take you. This will differ depending on the kind of animation you are using. For instance, if you are using drawn animation, your post-production stage will include the colouring of your film and will consequently take longer than if you were making a stop-motion film. Another example of where timings may differ is the backgrounds: they could be lavish and detailed or consist of only a few simple lines.

Once you have decided how long each aspect of film-making will take, you can draw up a schedule. As with budgeting, allow a little more time than you think you will need, so that you are well prepared for any emergencies that may occur. Here is an

	Week 1	Week 2	Week 3	Week 4	Week 5	Week 6	Week 7	Week 8	Week 9	Week 10
Script	■									
Character Design		■	■							
Background Design			■	■						
Storyboard			■	■						
Voice recording				▮						
Animation					■	■	■	■		
Sound effects									■	
Post-production										■

This is a ten-week schedule for making a short, 2D computer-animated film.

example of a ten-week-long schedule for making a 3-minute, 2D computer-animated film (above).

As you can see from this schedule, it is possible for different parts of the film-making process to overlap. For example, if you know that your film will be set in a medieval castle and feature mutant guinea pigs as knights in armour, someone can start working on backgrounds and character designs before the script is finalized. Sometimes you may be forced to break with the ideal order for making your film, starting to animate a scene before the background has been finished, for instance. Although a certain amount of flexibility may make your film quicker (and therefore cheaper) to make, it is important not to stray too far from the ideal order of doing things. For instance, any film-maker who starts animating before having completely finalized the character designs is bound to hit problems.

43

4 WRITING YOUR SCRIPT AND DESIGNING YOUR CHARACTERS

Script writing and character design are the most important parts of film-making to get right. A funny, clever, entertaining script will more than make up for any shortfalls in animation or general production quality. In fact, a good script combined with basic animation will always be more successful than a beautifully animated film with a bad script. *South Park* is a classic example of the former; the funny script keeps you watching some fairly rudimentary animation. Examples of the latter, nicely animated films without a decent script (or sometimes without a script at all) are seldom seen outside the studios or art schools which produced them.

Character design is a very different skill from script writing, but both are vital if your film is to have a sense of personality. This is important if your film is to have an emotional impact, rather than appearing as a series of events happening to a feature-less individual. A good script will make the protagonists in your film come across as real people, with their own quirks and weak-nesses; good character design will reflect these features and avoid your characters appearing bland or generic.

In this chapter we shall look at how to go about creating a script and characters that will enhance your film. We shall also look at

This bear is an unremarkable stereotype character...

... while this one is less perfect, but has more personality as a result.

how the two combine to give your film a unique, personal look.

Script Writing

Although this book is not intended to be a guide to script writing, there are several useful points which will help you to avoid problems when writing. In particular, these are designed to help you to avoid the pitfalls which may make your film impossible to animate.

Don't Write Animators into Corners

If you are writing a film with a limited budget and if you or the animators working on it have only limited experience, try to make concessions to this in your script. Try to avoid writing directions such as:

```
A tidal wave can be seen rushing
towards the beach. We can see the
wave through a window on the pier,
and, as it gets closer, we can see
hundreds of fish are caught up in
the wave, the sun reflecting off
their silver bellies. As the wave
crashes into the pier, the water
pours over every surface and smashes
into the arcade machines lining the
inside of the pier, shattering the
machines and sending waves of small
change spilling across the floor.
As the water from the wave ebbs
away through the gaps in the
pier's wooden floor, we see a mass
of fish and coins slowly slide
across the boards of the pier,
tipping over deckchairs and
glinting in the sun.
```

This script would take a huge amount of time to animate, and no little skill. Water is very tricky to animate well and the effort required to animate the movement of every single fish and coin would be extremely time-consuming. It is much better to identify anything that is too complicated to animate at the script stage rather than wait until you have spent two weeks attempting to animate it. But avoiding the complicated does not mean that you have to keep your ideas small. For example, the idea of a tidal wave hitting an English seaside town could be written like this:

```
Close up on a crazy golf course by
the seaside. SFX — a rushing, watery
noise. The golf course is suddenly
drenched by a huge wave, turning the
screen completely blue almost
immediately.

Fade to black. Fade up.

The golf course is covered in
puddles and a fish is stuck in one
of the holes.
```

This version still communicates the scale of events but it could be animated in an afternoon, whereas the previous version could take weeks.

Write Economically

Animation is time-consuming, and when you are making your own film you need to save as much time as possible. You can save a great deal at the script writing stage if you only write dialogue that is strictly necessary; do not be tempted to write more than you need since lines which take a few seconds to write could take hours to animate, without necessarily adding much to your film. For example, let us imagine that you are writing a scene in which two characters are planning a bank robbery and you want to show that one of them is much keener than the other. You could write:

```
DAVE
All set for the bank job tomorrow?
JULIAN
Well, I don't know, I'm a bit
worried …
DAVE
You can't pull out now!
JULIAN
I'm not pulling out, it's just that
I think I'm a bit busy tomorrow —
I've got the decorating to finish,
and …
DAVE
Look, we said tomorrow, so tomorrow
it is. End of.
JULIAN
But the skirting board does need a
final coat …
```

Alternatively, you could just write:

```
DAVE
All set for the bank job tomorrow?
JULIAN
Tuesday is my day for aqua-aerobics …
DAVE
See you at six. You muppet.
```

That gets the same information and characterization across in less than half the time.

Acting

Do not be too subtle It is best to avoid writing lines which rely on small, subtle, facial expressions to be acted out – the flicker of an eyebrow, for instance, or the twitch of a nostril. This is because few animated characters contain the detail required to show such emotions; if they did have this detail they would be almost impossible to animate. Even fairly realistic characters, such as those seen in Disney features, are simplified to make them easier to handle.

Exaggerate Although animated characters cannot convey all the tiny subtleties of human emotion, they can show a great range of emotions. The stupidity of Homer Simpson or the manic energy of Daffy Duck work well as animation, but they seem absurd if played by a live actor. Do not be afraid of writing characters that seem too dumb, too evil or too crazy for real life – animation is about exaggerating reality, not mimicking it.

Script Format

There is an accepted format for writing animation script. Although this may not seem to matter if you are writing a script for your own film, it is important to get it right if you ever want to submit a script to an animation company or television station. These people get hundreds of animation scripts sent to them and consequently they are always looking for a reason to avoid reading them to cut down on their workload. For this reason, most companies will refuse to read scripts which are not correctly formatted. However, the good news is that the format for animation scripts is not especially complicated, as the example overleaf shows.

Script format conventions

- character names are always written in capital letters
- sound effects are signified by writing SFX
- in animation a scene is the length of a shot between cuts; once you have cut to a different view you have started a new scene; this is different from live action, where a scene can contain several shots between cuts, as long as they are all

---

1. INT. LIVING ROOM. NIGHT

A paunchy, middle-aged man SAMUEL is crouched by an open window, along with his teenage son JUNIOR. SAMUEL is holding a huge baseball bat and JUNIOR is holding a table-tennis bat. A bored looking cat TABATHA is sitting on the sofa.

> SAMUEL (whisper)
> This time we've got him — as soon as he's through the window, he'll be getting this bat where he least expects it. And if he makes a break for it … well that's where your ping-pong bat comes into its own.
> JUNIOR (impressed, swinging the bat in practice)
> Sheer genius.

2. EXT. STREET. NIGHT.

A BURGLAR is sauntering along sizing up houses. SFX — distant sound of dog barking.

> BURGLAR
> Alarms, security gates, cameras … All powerless when faced with the greatest housebreaking tool known to man … Mwahahahahahaha!

He cackles evilly, and we zoom in on a tin of extremely posh-looking cat food in his pocket, labelled 'Golden Mush — cat food of kings!'

3. INT. LIVING ROOM. NIGHT.

TABATHA suddenly leaps up and freezes in a pose of crazed excitement. She then rushes to the door, unlocking and unbolting several locks in a frenzy of activity. SFX — noise of locks being opened. The door opens, and TABATHA leaps at the tin of cat food, which is now open. We see the BURGLAR's legs walk past into the house. The camera pulls out and the BURGLAR can be seen carrying out a huge range of furniture, including a grandfather clock. SAMUEL and JUNIOR are completely oblivious to all this activity happening behind their backs and remain poised for action by the open window.

> SAMUEL (under his breath)
> Any second now, son, any second now …

---

happening in the same place and at the same time.

CHARACTER DESIGN

Many people find character design the most appealing part of making an animated film. The design of the characters should sum up the spirit of your film; think of how *The Simpsons* is defined by its yellow characters with big eyes and an over-bite, or think of Aardman's distinctive characters in *Wallace and Gromit* with their wide mouths and expressive eyebrows.

This character would be rather tricky to animate ...

... but these simplifications would make it much easier.

The important point about character design is to remember that your final character will have to move. It is easy to become involved in your design work and end up with a character that looks great as an illustration but is hard to animate. There are several things you can do to prevent this from happening.

Don't Be Too Detailed

Every detail you create on a character drawing will have to be animated. This can make an apparently perfect character a nightmare to animate.

Curb your ambition Having to animate three spikes of hair instead of eleven will make your task far easier. Avoiding lettering at all costs will also save time; animating words rarely works – once the spaces in the lettering change even slightly the result will look wrong and catch the eye.

Base your characters on a simple construction Most of the best animated characters have had a fairly simple construction. Take the classic *Looney Tunes* characters, for example. Daffy Duck and Bugs Bunny both have the body of a simple cartoon human; Daffy is slightly shorter and has webbed feet and a beak, while Bugs is taller and has a cottontail and big ears and teeth. Apart from these characteristics, both characters are based on the same simple body, with no unnecessary details such as textured fur or feathers.

Use only the clothes you need In a live action film every character will have to wear a full set of clothes, full of hard-to-animate

49

This basic body design can be used for many types of character.

This character looks fine in a neutral position …

But his huge head and stubby arms make it hard to animate him eating.

details such as buttons, laces and zips. Fortunately, when it comes to animation we can discard any piece of clothing which does not help to communicate character. Having your characters half-naked may seem an odd idea, but it has been used in character design for years. Yogi Bear wears only a collar, a tie and a hat, while his little friend Boo-Boo wears just a bow tie. Top Cat wears only a waistcoat, Disney's Winnie the Pooh a simple shirt and Donald Duck the top half of a sailor's outfit (leaving out the troublesome bell-bottomed trousers). Even when characters are fully clothed the clothes can be simple, with characters wearing as few items as possible. Fred Flintstone wears a one-piece fur suit, which bears a passing resemblance to Lisa Simpson's simple orange dress.

Keep this tradition of half-clothed characters in mind when you design your character. Ask yourself whether every item of clothing your character is wearing is necessary, and if it is not then get rid of it.

Make a Character that Does What You Want It to Do

When designing a character it is important to draw it in positions that he or she is likely to take in the animation and not only in basic, neutral poses. This will allow you to spot any potential problems in animating your design before you actually begin to do so.

Your character does not have to be able to do everything, just the things that you need. This is one of the areas where script writing and character design overlap. Before starting your character design, read the script, even if it is not yet complete, and take note of the kinds of action the characters will be involved with. With the boy shown on page 50, it could be that he is meant to be a messenger boy and so will

This character's huge feet make it hard to animate him running since the feet get tangled up with the ground.

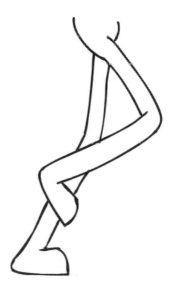

This character has smaller feet and it will be easier to animate runs as a result.

Every wrinkle and line on this face will need to be redrawn when the head moves.

This face has fewer lines and will be much easier to animate.

not need to be shown eating. In this case, the stubby arms would cease to be a problem, but it would be important for the character to be able to run quickly.

All successful animated characters have been designed to fit with the animation. For instance, the squashy bodies and elastic arms and legs of the *Looney Tunes* characters are ideally suited to the manic action they are involved in. Imagine trying to show the crazed energy of Daffy Duck if the character were drawn in the style of *South Park*.

Make Sure Your Character Fits with the Form of Animation

The kind of animation you are using should be considered when you are designing your characters. Designs which will work well for drawn animation could be problematic in model animation; characters from cut-out animation could be almost unworkable if drawn. The important points to consider

when designing characters for a particular form of animation are shown below.

Drawn animation The importance of not designing excessively detailed characters has already been stressed, but it should be noted that it is even more important when it comes to drawn animation. Every single line on your character will need to be redrawn for every frame in which your character moves, so be economical with your design: exclude lines you do not need.

It is also important to try to avoid lines which will be hard to animate. Often a wrinkle on a face or a line around the top of a dog's back leg will look fine in a design, but when animated it will take on a life of its own, appearing to jump and wriggle independently of the rest of your animation. This most frequently happens with lines that sit inside the character outline, such as the creases in a rhino's hide, for example.

The lines on this rhino will have a tendency to wriggle and catch the eye when animated.

This simpler rhino has fewer lines and will be easier to animate.

3D animation 3D animation should be the least limiting of all types of animation to design characters for, since the computer environment allows you to avoid many of the practical difficulties found in drawn or model work. However, designing characters for the 3D environment does have some important restrictions. The first of these relates to the abilities of your character modeller. Modelling characters in 3D is a special skill that takes a long time to perfect.

Make sure that you do not end up drawing a character that is hard to model. As a general rule, the more complex the shape of a character and the more parts it has, then the harder it will be to model.

The second restriction is that 3D characters are built as skeletons and then animated by moving the parts of that skeleton. It is important to remember this if you are designing a character that has a flexible shape and form which frequently changes.

Making your character squash or distort can be time-consuming in 3D animation since it often necessitates the remodelling of the whole character. This was part of the reason why Pixar used toys for its first feature since they were wooden or plastic and therefore inflexible and hence rarely distorted or changed shape.

Cut-out/2D computer animation Cut-out, or the version of it which is often used in 2D computer animation, allows you to design characters with much more detail than other ways of working. Because you are moving existing drawings of body parts around, rather than recreating them in every frame, it is possible to have more complicated designs. Of course, this will give your animation a particular stylized look, with little or no follow-through animation – heads will move, but hair will stay in place undisturbed. However, as cut-out animation is highly stylized in the first place, this will not look out of place. If a similar style of animation were tried in model or 3D animation – both of which are technically suited to the moving around of complicated but unchanging body parts – it could look out of place since these ways of working are more often used for more realistic animation.

Model animation When designing characters for model animation the problems you face are not so much creative as practical. You need to create a character that will be

The geometric shapes which make up this mouse will be easy to model in a 3D environment.

This mouse is made up of more complicated shapes and so will be harder to model.

able to stand up and move without falling over. You also need to consider the durability of your character: will it include lots of tiny details which will easily break off and need frequent replacement? This is why characters in model animation always look solid and well built. There is no point in trying to move a character which cannot even stand up!

Create a Model Sheet

Once you have designed a suitable character it is important to create a model sheet. A model sheet shows exactly what that character looks like from every angle. This is vital if your character is to stay 'on model'.

'On model' means making sure that your character always looks exactly the same and

This monster's head may be moved as one cut-out piece, which means that it can look quite complex.

A model of this character will not be able to stand up since its huge beak will cause it to topple over. Its detailed wings will be flimsy and easily break off.

A model of this character will be much easier to work with.

This model sheet shows the character from every angle. The lines on the sheet show how the character is proportioned.

does not change nor distort as you animate. Although this is not a problem when you use computers, it is one of the hardest things to get right in other forms of animation. As the character is redrawn or moved to create a new frame, it is easy for tiny changes in the character to appear. The neck might get fractionally longer or the nose slightly smaller. Although this one change might not be noticeable, if the same thing happens over several frames then, within a couple of seconds, a character may change completely. Model sheets can be used to avoid this.

They are also useful if you have more than one animator working on a film. Even if each one is given a drawing of a character, there will be many different ways of interpreting that drawing and you could find your character's appearance changing from animator to animator. Model sheets give animators a clear reference point for every possible angle, allowing everyone's animation to stay on model. To help the animators keep the characters on model, model sheets often include tips on what to do and what not to do when drawing particular parts of the body.

Including tips like this on a model sheet will help animators to keep characters on model.

Combining Character Design and Script – Rules for Your Film

Although character design and script writing are two quite separate parts of film-making, they are closely related when it comes to determining the rules of your film. These will decree what your characters can and cannot do – not in terms of the plot but in terms of animation. For instance, are you making the kind of film where, if a character walks off a cliff, he walks a few steps beyond the cliff edge before standing still in mid-air, looking round in confusion and panic, then finally plummeting to the ground? Or is your film one where cliff-top falls are instantaneous, not to mention bloody and painful? These rules lie somewhere between script writing and character design and affect both of them, so they are important to get right before you start animating.

Exaggeration – how cartoony is your film? As in the example above, many of the rules of your film will deal with how 'cartoony' your film is. Another way of putting this is to note that all animation exaggerates reality, but not to the same extent. Some animation makes a virtue of extreme exaggeration – Tex Avery's *Wolf* films for MGM are a good example: on seeing the pretty young girl, Wolf would hover in mid-air, his heart pounding so that it almost burst through his jacket, eyes bulging or turning into hearts. In contrast, *The Simpsons* deliberately steered away from this kind of exaggeration, keeping the characters much more realistic. What is important with both examples is that the level of exaggeration is consistent; Wolf always reacts wildly, and the Simpsons always react realistically.

You can keep your character realistic …

… or exaggerate somewhat …

… or exaggerate a lot!

57

5   STORYBOARDS, LAYOUTS AND ANIMATICS

Directing animation is quite different from directing a live action film. Directing live action is very hands-on – you watch every stage of your film being created and can give instructions and suggestions at any point in the filming. This is obviously not possible when directing an animated film. One problem is that there could be several animators working on different scenes at the same time. When Aardman animation made *Chicken Run* they used two directors to help to deal with this. But the bigger problem when directing animation is that, unless you are animating the entire film yourself, at some point you simply have to let your animators get on and animate; it is not possible to direct them at every step of the way. You could try looking over their shoulders at their drawings or computer monitor every minute of the day, but it will tire you out, annoy your animators and achieve little. There are much better ways of ensuring that your animators produce the animation you are after by using storyboards, layouts and animatics.

WHAT ARE STORYBOARDS, LAYOUTS AND ANIMATICS?

Storyboards are series of pictures telling the story of your film and all the action in it. The drawings for storyboards are smaller and simpler versions of the artwork which will appear in your film. By referring to the storyboard everyone working on the film will know what is supposed to happen and the order it happens in.

Layouts are full-size, more precise versions of storyboard drawings. They show exactly where everything in a scene should go and also where the light in the scene is coming from. They are used by background artists and animators to place characters and other elements in a scene.

An *animatic* is a full-length version of your final film prepared from the layout drawings. By putting all the layout drawings on for the right number of frames it is possible to get an idea of how the finished film will look before you begin work on the animation. An animatic will let you check and adjust the timing; it will show you whether a scene is too quick or too slow. Animatics are sometimes called *Leicas*, after the brand of camera originally used to film them.

STORYBOARDS

Detail
The art of good storyboards is knowing the right level of detail to include. If you include too little, then your animators will be confused and you may not end up with the film you wanted. Alternatively, if you produce storyboards which are as detailed and complete as is humanly possible, you will end by devoting a great deal of time to artwork

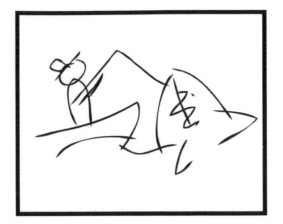

This panel is too rough to be clearly understood.

This panel is clear but it contains much unnecessary detail.

This panel is not overly detailed but it is clear enough to be understood.

which will not appear in your final film. The smaller details of the character design will be covered by model sheets and the finer points of background images are better left until the layout stage. The ideal storyboard lies somewhere in between: not too rough as to be unclear to anyone doing animation, layout or backgrounds, but not containing any unnecessary detail either.

The amount of detail you include in your storyboard will also be affected by those to whom you are intending to show it. If you are animating and laying out the film yourself, you can afford to be fairly rough when drawing your storyboards; as long as you can understand them that is all that matters. However, sometimes you may find yourself wanting to show storyboards to people in an attempt to get funding for your film. If this is the case, then it is better to make your storyboards look as impressive as possible, even if it means spending time drawing in detail which is not strictly necessary.

Size

There is no set size for storyboard drawings, although they tend to be small to avoid unnecessary detail. Some animators even do tiny thumbnail sketches for storyboards; this forces them to concentrate on the bare essentials of the characters' poses, without being distracted by worry about how the drawing actually looks. Thumbnail drawings are also much quicker to draw.

You could draw your storyboard panels this size ...

... but this thumbnail is quicker to draw and contains all the information required.

Timing

When you begin to draw a storyboard it may be hard to know how many drawings to do. As with detail, you need to strike a balance: if you do too few drawings there will be large intervals of time between panels. This means that the animators working on your film will have to use their own imagination and creativity to fill these gaps. Although this can be helpful since it brings fresh ideas to your film, the obvious disadvantage is that it will mean your losing a degree of control over what your finished film will look like. The alternative is to storyboard every single movement in your film,

which could mean drawing two or three panels for every second. This would give you almost total control over what your animators do, but it would also mean devoting almost as much time to storyboarding the film as animating it. This is not a good idea because, although storyboards are important, they will only ever be seen by your animators; your animation will be seen by everyone watching your film.

It would make life easier if there were a firm rule of thumb which could be used when drawing storyboards; for example, drawing one panel for every five seconds of action. Unfortunately, this is not possible

This sword fight needs three panels to describe less than a second's worth of action.

Television Formats — Frame Rates and Size

When working with animation you will often hear people refer to the length of a scene or a movement as a number of frames. Frames are the units of time that make up one second; part of the skill of learning animation is getting to know how long ten frames feels and what would happen if you changed a hold from six frames to fourteen. This can take some time and is made more complicated by the fact that different formats have different frame rates; that is, if you are making your film to be shown on video in the USA it will have a different number of frames per second, or frame rate, than if you were making it to be shown in the United Kingdom.

Just as different formats have different frame rates, they also have different sizes. As with frame rates, it is important to make sure that you know what dimensions your finished film will have. The accompanying table shows the frame rates and size of different formats.

Thinking about Frame Rates

As much animation is done holding an image for two frames, it is easier to think of a second of animation containing an even number of frames. It is perfectly reasonable to think of PAL having twenty-four frames per second for the purpose of animating, even though it is actually twenty-five. However, do not forget to get the frame rate right when producing the final cut of your film.

Square and Non-square Pixels

Computer and television images are made up of pixels, thousands of tiny blocks of colour which come together to make an image. Pixels in computers are square, but pixels on PAL video and most digital video are slightly oblong in shape; they are referred to as 'non-square pixels'. This means that, if you import digital video footage into a computer, it will look slightly different, although the image has not been altered and will look as was intended when shown on a video screen. However, if you are creating your images in a computer to begin with, then images created with the same pixel dimensions as PAL video will not

since the number of panels you need will depend on the action you are storyboarding. If you are drawing a storyboard for a fast-paced scene with lots of action, you might find yourself drawing a panel for every eight or ten frames. On the other hand, a storyboard for a scene featuring a close-up of two characters talking might need only one panel for ten seconds of action.

LEFT: *This conversation could last for several seconds but would still only need one panel in the storyboard.*

Television Formats

Format	Frame rate per second	Size in pixels
NTSC video (used in the USA, Canada and Japan)	30	640 × 480
PAL video (used in Europe)	25	720 × 576
PAL wide screen (Europe)	25	1024 × 576
ATSC wide screen (North America)	30	1280 × 720 or 1920 × 1080
film	24	no set size, but the bigger the image the better the quality.

look the same on the television screen as they do on the computer monitor. They will be slightly distorted and the edges of shapes may also look a little jagged.

This problem can be avoided by working with computer images which are slightly wider than PAL video size and then converting them to PAL size once they have been completed. To do this, your computer images need to be 768 × 576 and then to be exported at 720 × 576. NTSC formats and PAL wide screen use square pixels, which saves your having to make this adjustment.

Always make sure that you know the size of the format you are working in and the size at which your final film will be shown in. If in doubt, talk to whoever is going to produce the finished version of your film, be it a friend or a company, and ask for their advice.

LAYOUTS

Layouts provide your final chance to make it absolutely clear what you want from your animators. As layouts are bigger than storyboards, they can be more detailed; a good layout should include every piece of information an animator needs for a scene. The proportions of the characters in relation to the background, the direction of any light falling on a character and the perspective of the scene as a whole should all be included.

Layouts are all about communication; they allow a director to tell an animator exactly what he or she wants from a scene. If you are making a film with a very small team (one director, one writer and one animator, for example) it may well be that layouts are unnecessary since the director will be able to talk the animator through what is required using the storyboard. However, as soon as you begin to work with a small team of animators you will find that it becomes much harder for the director to discuss every scene with every animator, and layout drawings become an invaluable way of making it clear what the animator needs to do.

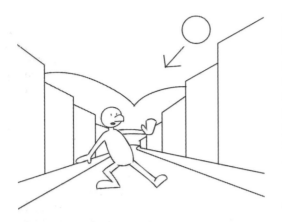

This layout drawing shows the animator the character pose and position as well as the source of the light falling on the character. The drawing can also be used by the background artist to get the right perspective.

Layouts in Non-Computer Animation

In drawn animation layouts are drawn on the same sized paper as that used for animation. This means that the animator can trace over the layout drawing to make sure everything is in the right place. Obviously this is not possible in stop-motion animation. However, layouts are even more important when doing stop-motion work since it is not possible to use key frames when animating. This means that the layout drawings together with the storyboard provide the only way of planning your animation.

Layouts in Computer Animation

The advantage of computer animation is that, instead of just giving your animators a layout on paper which they need to study and reproduce in their own animation, you can set out a scene in the computer ready for your animators to work with straightaway. For example, in 3D animation you could position the lights and the camera exactly where you want them and even set up the character model in the correct starting pose. In 2D computer animation you could similarly place everything in the right position on screen ready to be animated.

ANIMATICS

Once you have created your layout making your animatic is straightforward. All you need to do is film your drawings in order, holding them for the length of time that they are meant to represent. An animatic without sound is still useful although once you have the dialogue recorded then it is well worth adding it too. If you are not doing layout drawings you can film the storyboard panels instead. Watching the resulting, unanimated version of your film should show you whether or not the scenes and timing you have planned will work. This is sometimes described as seeing how an animated film 'reads'.

When watching an animatic it is important not to be distracted by the lack of animation but instead to concentrate on the action and the ideas that are being communicated, and to ask yourself whether they are coming across clearly. The best way of seeing whether your film is working is to find someone who knows nothing about it and show them the animatic. Once they have watched it, ask them to tell you what happened in it. It is very important to pay attention to what they tell you. When someone says that they do not understand a part of it, it is all too easy to lay the blame on them rather than face the fact that your film may be less than clear.

Safety

Making sure that your animated images are clearly visible on a television screen is referred to as making them 'TV safe'. Keeping your film TV safe refers to the colour of your animation and where it appears on the screen.

Colour

Computer screens show colour as a mixture of red, green and blue. Each colour is assigned a value between 0 and 255. This system is called RGB. Television screens show colour in a less sophisticated way, so that something which looks bright and colourful on a computer may look murky and muddy on television. More importantly, very bright colours that look good on a computer may be blurred and wobble on a television screen.

This blurring happens with colours that are fully saturated; that is, ones that go to the extremes of the scales for red, green and blue. For instance, if you use a red that has an RGB value of red: 255, green: 0 and blue: 0 it will blend into neighbouring colours when viewed on television, especially if those colours are also fully saturated. To avoid this you need to move the values away from the extremes by about 15 points or so. For instance, the red we were using before would be changed to a value of 240, green to 15 and blue to 15.

Area

Not everything that appears on a computer screen or a camera will be visible on television. TV screens cut off the edges of your picture and different screens cut off different amounts; but to make sure that everyone can see your animation properly it is best to work with a safety guide. This will indicate a safe area within which you should keep all the important action of your film. It is also a good idea to use what is called a title safe area. This is an area further away from the edge of the screen than the general safe area and is used for any writing that appears on screen. It is a smaller area because it is vital that any writing on screen is readable, whereas if a small part of a character strays off screen it is less important. If you are using drawn animation you can buy a graticule, a transparent cel with safety guides on. However, it is quite easy to create a basic guide your self – use the one below as an example.

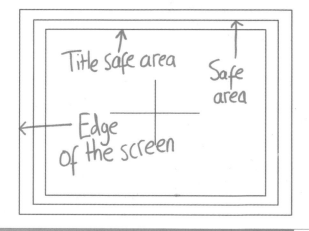

A television safety guide, showing the general safe area and title safe area.

Make sure that you show your animatic to everyone working on the film. It will give them an idea of its tone and pace, which may be hard to judge from the storyboard and script alone, and this will add to the animation in your finished film.

DIRECTING

So far in this chapter we have looked at the practical ways a director of an animated film can communicate what he or she wants to the animators. The creative side of directing is far less easy to pin down since there are as many different ways of directing animation as there are animated films. The following are general rules to bear in mind when directing. However, do not feel bound by them – go with what feels right for your film. Good directors almost always break at least one rule.

Directing Animation Is Not Like Directing Live Action Films

This is obvious, but it is worth restating because, however much animation you may have watched, the vast majority of films and television programmes you will have seen are bound to have been live action, and this will inevitably have influenced how you think about directing. This is not a problem so long as you remember that not everything that works in live action will work in animation. In particular:

Stay away from flashy camera work The average live action film will contain all sorts of different camera tricks: a shaky camera to make things look more gritty and realistic; very quick cuts to show memory flashbacks; a camera whizzing between characters involved in a stand-off. These things rarely work as well in animation as they do in live action. In a live action film these camera tricks take a real life scene and exaggerate or abstract it. Animation, on the other hand, is already an exaggeration and abstraction of reality; add too many tricks to it and it starts to become unclear.

Avoid extreme close-ups Live action films often make use of close-ups of a character's face, frequently showing just the eyes, particularly in moments of high stress or tension. These close-ups are not often successful in animation. An animated character is a simplified version of a real person and so does not have the detail which can be seen in an extreme close-up in live action, such as pores, eyelashes or veins under the skin. A close-up of the eyes of an animated character can start to look like a set of abstract shapes, making your film seem less believable.

Keep Things Looking Lively

When making an animated film it is important not to get so immersed in your animation that you forget camera work entirely. A long scene of, say, thirty seconds, will look static and slightly dull if it all takes place in the same shot. Try showing a close-up of a character when he speaks or, alternatively, have a slow camera zoom taking place for the entire length of the scene. Not only will this make the film seem more lively, it could save you work when it comes to animating. If you include close-ups of the head and shoulders of a character you will not have to animate the entire body.

Keep Things Clear

As already mentioned, animation is an exaggeration and abstraction of reality. This means that it may be somewhat hard for the viewer to follow; thus it is important to do everything to make things as clear as possible to the eyes of your audience.

Character poses Character poses are always clearer if they present a good, clearly outlined shape. It is best to think of what the pose would look like if it were a silhouette – the clearer the silhouetted image is, the better the pose.

The idea of using silhouettes began with early Disney characters such as Mickey Mouse. The original Mickey was entirely black, with no outline around him; this meant that, when his arm was over his body, it was impossible to see where it was. This led the Disney animators to adopt the process of using good silhouettes, a practice they found worked equally well with characters which had outlines.

Do not get carried away with camera moves Although camera moves can help your film to look lively, it is important not to

This pose makes a very confusing silhouette.

This pose shows the same action but it makes a much clearer silhouette and so will be easier to read when animated.

Camera Terms

Cut	An abrupt change, where one shot on screen is instantly replaced by another.
Crosscutting	Cutting quickly back and forth between two events, creating the impression that they are happening at the same time.
Fade	Image slowly fades away from the screen; this is often done as a Fade to Black where the images fades into a black screen.
Long shot	A shot showing everything in the scene in full.
Medium shot	A shot showing characters from the waist up; you can also show objects or parts of the background in medium shots.
Close-up	A shot showing a character's face; you can also have close-ups on objects or parts of the background.
Pan	The camera moves across to show a different part of a scene.
Track	The camera moves sideways, keeping pace with a moving character or object.
Zoom	The camera smoothly changes to make objects appear closer or further away.

use too many of them. In particular, try to avoid zooming in, out, then in again, then cutting out to a long shot, then zooming in for a third time. This will not add much to your film, but it will make your audience feel more than a little queasy.

Do not cross the line 'Crossing the line' is a cut which takes the camera through 180 degrees. Although this may be dramatic, more often than not it is confusing since it causes the viewer to lose track of where he or she is in the scene.

This cut is possible, but it could be confusing.

This cut is much clearer since it does not cross the line.

Keep Encouraging People

One of the most important parts of directing any film is to keep everyone working on the film motivated and enthusiastic. In live action films there are many stories of great directors who have been tough, unreasonable and almost unbearable to work with, but who have still produced great work. This style of directing is much less likely to work in animation. This is because the live action director will often be filming only two or three minutes worth of film in a day, and so, no matter how angry or abusive he or she is, as long as the actors and technicians can be persuaded to come up with the goods for those few minutes, a good film can be produced. In animation the people making your film will be working on it solidly all day and a director needs to coax a good performance out of them for the whole time. If you attempt to achieve this by shouting at and belittling your animators then you will reduce their confidence and their work rate, neither of which will do your film any good. A good animation director will still criticize the animators' work when necessary, but he or she will also understand the importance of encouraging everyone on the film to do their absolute best.

69

6   VOICE RECORDING AND BACKGROUNDS

Voice recording and background work are, more often than not, the last things you do before you start animating. There are good reasons for this. The equipment and people you use for your voice recording are unlikely to be involved in other parts of the film, and may be costly. This means that, while you get frequent chances to rework your script and animation, you will often have only one chance to get a voice recording right. This in turn means that you need your voice recording session to be as productive as possible; you should record voices only when your script and storyline are completely finalized.

Backgrounds appear at this late stage in the schedule for a more straightforward reason – apart from the actual animation, few if any other parts of making an animated film are dependent on completed backgrounds. The script, character design, storyboard and animatic can all be worked on before the backgrounds are complete, and so backgrounds tend to be the last thing that is finished. In this chapter we shall look at how to produce voice recordings and backgrounds which will enhance your film.

BACKGROUNDS

Animation backgrounds are free from many of the restrictions affecting animated characters. Backgrounds can be completely still, meaning that it is possible to make them much more detailed than animation. For example, the backgrounds in Tex Avery's classic *Droopy* films or those in *Tom and Jerry* are painted with a depth and subtlety far beyond the flat colours and outlines of the characters which appear in front of them.

This difference leads to another important option for backgrounds: they need not be in the same style as the animation. Although many television series use the same style of drawing for both the animation and the backgrounds – *The Simpsons*, for example, or *King of the Hill* – this is not the only way of doing things. *Dangermouse*, for example, used collages of famous London buildings for backgrounds, while the characters were in a more typically cartoony, flat, coloured style.

Avoid Distraction

Although background artwork can be more detailed and varied than character artwork, it is important to remember that a good background should show your animation in the best possible light. It is easy to forget this when working on a background and end up producing something which works well as an illustration, but distracts viewers from your finished animation.

Put detail only where it is needed Not every area of your background will require the same level of detail. In general, you

Copyright

There is no need to be confined to using your own drawings for backgrounds – you could use any type of image, from photo collages to Renaissance paintings to create the effect you are after. However, if you are going to use images other than your own, then you need to be aware of the rules of copyright. This is the law that protects the expression of ideas; it is not something that has to be registered or written down, but something that exists as soon as someone has painted a picture, composed music, written a story or made a film. The person responsible for creating the work of art automatically owns the copyright.

However, the copyright of a piece of art automatically runs out seventy years after the death of its creator. This means that you could create a film played out against a background of old master paintings for free. But there are catches which you need to be aware of; although an old painting may be out of copyright, the colour photograph of it that you are using will probably still be in copyright. There are three ways of getting round this. First, you could take your own photograph of the painting; this could be difficult since the gallery possessing it could be at the other side of the world, and, if and when you get there, it is quite likely that photography would not be allowed. Secondly, you could try to find a copyright-free image of the painting. Photographers and artists sometimes waive their copyright in exchange for a fee from publishers, who then produce books of copyright-free images. Thirdly, you could rework the photograph of the paint-ing, tracing it or adjusting it in Photoshop, so that it becomes your own version of the original.

Copyright will also have a big impact on your own work; you will need to make sure that your film is not pirated by someone else. To prevent this from happening it is important to understand that copyright does not protect ideas, but their expression. This means that if you think of a great idea for a film but then do nothing with it, you have no copyright over that idea. Even if someone makes a film which is exactly like your idea you will have no way of proving that you thought of it first, and no rights over an idea you did nothing with. However, if you write a script or draw a storyboard, then you automatically have copyright over that work. In the unlikely event of someone stealing your work, you will need to be able to prove when you created it. The best way to do this is to register the script of your film with a reputable organization, often a writers' guild or an animation trade union. Once your script has been registered the organization you have registered it with will be able to prove exactly when it was created. The Writers Guild of America provides a script registra-tion service for a small fee; in Britain, BECTU, the animation union, provides the same service.

It is worth remembering that, although all creative people worry about having their work stolen, it is in practice some-thing that rarely happens. A good under-standing of copyright will make it even less likely to occur. (*See* Chapter 8 to see how copyright affects music.)

In thls background, the castle distracts the viewer, taking the eye away from the characters.

Here the castle is more understated, letting the audience concentrate on the characters.

should concentrate the detail of your background around your characters. If you are animating a countryside scene, then the field your characters are standing in and the fence they are leaning against can be quite detailed, but the hillside in the distance behind them could be very simple, consisting of a flat shape silhouetted against the sky. This will prevent the viewer's eye being distracted by something which has nothing to do with the action taking place.

Use your background to focus attention on your characters As well as avoiding the

problems of distraction, you can actually use your background to help your audience to concentrate on your animation. This can be done by making sure that the elements in your background all lead the eye towards the characters. This will make it clear what part of the scene your audience should be watching.

Make Sure Your Backgrounds Work

As well as avoiding the problems discussed above, it is also important to ensure that your background technically works with

This background distracts the eye and draws it away from the characters.

your animation. This means different things according to the type of animation you are doing.

Drawn animation When using drawn animation you need to make sure that your background does not contain any elements that will need to be animated later on. Any object which will be affected by your characters or any other aspects in your film needs to be on a separate layer from the background. This could include a cup your characters drink from, a rake they walk into or a pair of socks on a washing line blowing in the breeze. As well as these objects being on separate layers, they may need to be drawn in a different style from other background elements so that they will be easier to animate. Objects being used by your characters will need to be drawn in the style

of them, rather than in the style of your background.

The same applies to backgrounds in cut-out animation and to a certain extent to those in 2D computer animation.

Model animation The main difference with model animation is that your backgrounds will actually exist in real space. You need to bear this in mind when planning your background and make sure you do not end designing something that cannot be built, or something which can be built but which also wobbles and shakes. You also need to build a background which gives you enough space in which to get hold of and move your characters. For example, if you are building a room, you might want to leave it open at the top so that you can reach inside to move the characters; this

Here the buildings draw the eye towards the characters.

will also give you a wider range of camera angles. If you want to include a ceiling or a roof in a set, make it one which is easy to take off if this is necessary.

It is also important to make sure that you have the scale right when building model backgrounds. It is best to complete your characters before beginning work on the background; in this way you can avoid building a chair too small for your character to sit in or a table too high for him to eat at.

3D animation Creating backgrounds for 3D animation involves some, but obviously not all, of the limitations of model animation. Although you do not need to worry about having enough room to move your characters, you do need to make sure that your background contains sufficient space for your characters to move around in. It is

also useful to think about the angle your background is going to be viewed from before you start building it. The great temptation with all 3D animation is to create the background or the animation and then to move the cameras around to try to find a suitable angle to show them at. It is much better to decide on the angle before you start work, since this means that you can design every part of the background to look good from that angle.

VOICE RECORDING

The most difficult part of voice recording is finding the right voice for your characters. As mentioned earlier, it is worth making use of any friends or family who are good with voices; however, if this is unsuccessful, you may need to seek out voice artists. A useful list of specialist animation voice artists may be found in Animation UK; try AWN Global Animation Business Directory for artists outside Britain. Another possibility is to approach local drama schools; you might be able to find an aspiring actor prepared to help you for little or no money in exchange for some useful experience.

Matching Your Voices to Your Film

The kinds of voice you are looking for will depend greatly on the feel you want your film to have. For example, if you were making an animated version of *Romeo and Juliet*, using exquisitely detailed animation, you would probably want voice artists who can deliver serious, actorly performances – this may well mean using a trained actor instead of one of your friends. On the other hand, if your film is down to earth and funny, your friends' untrained, everyday voices could work well, and be even better than using an actor. The ultimate example of this approach was Aardman's *Creature Comforts*, which used unscripted interviews with the public to provide voice-overs for zoo animals. Much of the humour in the films came from the contrast between the characters and the voices, with hefty gorillas speaking like quiet old ladies. This is an approach worth considering when casting voices for your film; instead of going for voices which emphasize the obvious characteristics of your character, try something unexpected. If you are animating a superhero, give him a quiet, Geordie accent rather than the bland American one your audience might expect.

Try to get hold of an impressionist It is hugely useful if one of the people on your film can do impressions of several different voices. This means that he or she can be used to voice several, or even all, the char-

acters in the film, saving you time, money and bother. Many of the best animation shows have used the same voice-over artist to do more than one character. The most famous example of this was Mel Blanc's work on the *Looney Tunes* films, where he did the voices for Woody Woodpecker, Daffy Duck, Foghorn Leghorn and Bugs Bunny. A similar thing happens in *The Simpsons*, where Dan Castellaneta does the voices for Homer, Granpa Simpson, Barney and groundskeeper Willie.

Recording Your Voices

Good sound quality is vital It is important to make sure that the sound quality of your voice recording is as good as possible. A clear, well-recorded soundtrack will help your film in two ways. First, and most obviously, it will make it easier for your audience to understand. Just as clearly posed, silhouetted characters make your film easier to watch, a well-recorded voice track will make it easier to understand. Secondly, a good quality voice track will improve every aspect of your film, not just the voices. A crackly, poorly recorded track creates the impression that your film as a whole is of low quality; people start looking for mistakes in the animation, or, worse, turn off completely because it sounds so bad.

Making a recording To get a good quality recording, it is always best to go to a professional recording studio. This does not have to be as expensive as it may sound; local telephone directories are full of small sound studios which can be hired out by the hour. If you are making a five-minute film, then an hour should be more than enough time to do a recording. However, as you will be paying for your time in the studio, you need to do everything you can to keep that time to a minimum. It is worth

Sound Software Packages

Making a voice track consists of two stages: recording and editing. The main package used for recording is Pro Tools. This allows you to record good quality sound which can then be edited at home or in the animation studio. Although cheap by the traditional standards of sound equipment, it is still quite costly for a facility which will be used only once in the film-making process. Most recording studios will have their own recording software and will usually be able to put you in touch with a producer who can operate it for you. Editing the sound – breaking down your original recording into separate scenes and selecting the takes you want – can be done with any basic sound package. Cool Edit, Audition and Sound Forge are three examples, but any program which lets you cut and paste sound files will do.

But whichever package you use it is best to save your sound in a format which can be used in as many different programs as possible. This means saving it as either a wav or an MP3. MP3s compress sound to keep the file size as small as possible, so it is generally better to use wavs. However, if you will be emailing sound files to people animating your film or if you are importing sound direct into a computer animation file, a small file size could be useful.

running through your script a few times before you get into the studio so that everyone knows what is required. It is also a good idea to do the sound editing out of the studio on a home computer – basic sound editing software is much cheaper than the packages required to make good sound recordings (*see* above for sound software packages).

Of course, it is possible to do sound recording at home. However, this is worth doing only if you are seriously interested in getting involved in the sound recording side of film-making. It requires costly software and hardware, and could, depending on where you live, mean spending large sums on soundproofing. Remember that, although you may work on your film for weeks or even months, the voice-recording session is likely to last for only an hour, and so, unless you are serious about doing more sound recording in future, it does not make sense to spend time and money setting up a home studio.

Directing the Sound Recording

Directing a sound recording is all about communicating with your voice artists, making sure that they know exactly what you want. Once that is clear, it is best to sit back and let them get on with it. It is advisable to resist the temptation to try to dictate precisely how every line is read. Voice artists will almost always bring their own ideas to a script and it is often better to go along with their interpretation than to try to enforce your own. Remember that the reason you are using voice artists in the first place is because they can do something – a voice, an accent, acting – which you cannot.

There are two other points worth noting when directing a voice recording. First, if you have someone doing the voices for more than one character, let him or her record all of a character's lines in one session. This will make it easier for the voice artist to give the character the same voice throughout the film; in turn, this will make

Sound	Action	Frame Numbers	Levels						Camera
			Top					Bottom	
G	GOOD	1							
		2							
O		3							
O		4							
		5							
		6							
		7							
D		8							
		9							
		10							
M	MORNING	11							
		12							
		13							
O		14							
R		15							
		16							
		17							
		18							
N		19							
		20							
I		21							
N		22							
G		23							
		24							
		25							
		26							
		27							

The breakdown on this dope sheet shows where each sound falls in the scene. For example, the word 'morning' begins in frame 11.

it easier for people to follow your film. If you go through the script in sequence, making your voice artist switch between characters, the accents may get mixed up. Mel Blanc used to record his voice parts by switching from character to character, but he was a genius and was working with well-established character voices. Your character voices will have only just been created and so it will be harder for your voice artist to keep a hold on them.

Secondly, make sure that you record the whole of the recording session. It is much easier to record too much and then edit it down. The alternative, where you record only takes, having rehearsed them off mike, leads to wasted time in trying to recreate the feel of a line or an improvisation that sounded perfect in rehearsal.

Editing and Breaking Down Voice Recordings

Once you have your finished sound recording, you need to edit it with a sound software package (*see* the box on page 77). The aim of editing is to break your recording down into a separate sound file for each scene. To do this, you will need to listen to your recording with a copy of the script or storyboard to hand, then cut and paste the versions of the scene you want into new files. Although this process may sound rather mundane, it can be quite creative. You can mix lines from different takes of a scene to create a new version and change the space between lines to add tension or comedy.

Producing a breakdown Unless you are importing your sound directly into a computer animation file, you will need to produce what is called a 'breakdown'. This is a written version of your recording which maps out exactly which frame every sound appears in. You will need one for every scene containing lip-synch or acting with dialogue in your film, and also for any scenes set in time to music. Without it, it will be impossible to animate in time with words and sounds.

Breakdowns may be included on a dope sheet, but they are sometimes put on to separate breakdown sheets. Dope sheets run from top to bottom, while breakdown sheets run from left to right, but, other than that, the information shown is identical (*see* Chapter 2 for more on dope sheets).

To create a breakdown of your recording you need to scroll very slowly through your sound, checking the frame number that each sound begins on. Some find it easier to find the starting frames for the words first and then go back and find the frame numbers for the individual sounds. Producing breakdowns can be painstakingly slow to start with, but you will soon pick up speed. Once you have finished, you are ready to start animating.

7 ANIMATION

As stated in Chapter 1, this book does not aim to be an exhaustive guide to all the skills required to be a top animator. It is about the practicalities of making an animated film. This is a task that will often need to be completed within a few short months or even weeks, due to the restrictions of time and money. In contrast, mastering all the skills of animation is something that can take years or even decades. While not attempting to condense years of experience into a few pages, this chapter will try to deal with the common problems faced by animators working on their first film. By laying out the key principles of timing, movement and acting, as well as including some useful tips and tricks, it should save you much time spent working things out for yourself. The first and most important aspect of animation we shall look at is timing.

TIMING

Timing is the most important part of animation to get right. This is because it is timing that makes animation actually animate. If you get the timing badly wrong, then the illusion of movement begins to break down; your audience becomes aware that they are watching a sequence of still images, not one moving picture. Timing is also what makes a film funny or moving – the pause before a piano falls on someone's head or the time it takes someone to realize that his dog has died; all of this needs good

timing to work. Even when there is no movement on screen you need a good sense of timing to know how long a sign should be on screen to be readable or how long to hold an opening long shot of a city landscape.

Timing of Movements
When you begin to animate it may be hard to know how long a movement should take. For instance, you may pick up and drink from a mug of tea several times a day, but could you say how long that movement takes?

Starting too quickly When you start to animate for the first time it is easy to get carried away and try to do too much in too short a period. People are not used to dealing with the fractions of a second that matter to animation, and when you are starting out it is easy to think of thirty-five frames as a long time. In fact, it is only just over a second. If you try to animate a move in too short a period, your animation can become unreadable.

Even if the space between your images is small enough to create the illusion of movement, it is still possible for a move to be too quick. This is particularly the case if you are trying to communicate something unusual or unexpected; your audience needs time to take in and understand a movement, not just register it as a fleeting blur across the screen.

Attempting to animate this move with only three drawings will not work. The drawings are too far apart to trick the eye into thinking that it is seeing a single movement. Furthermore, if the move were shot on twos, it would take only six frames (a quarter of a second), which is clearly far too quick.

You can tell your moves are going too quickly if you need to watch them three or four times to understand what is happening. A problem with all animation is that animators tend to watch their work hundreds of times over, while an audience watches it only once. It is always worth finding someone who has not seen any of your film, show them a scene once and then ask what they thought happened. If they get it wrong or they are not quite certain, then it is quite likely that your timing is too fast.

Going too slowly Once you have animated a few images and start to get a feel for how short a time one frame of animation is, it is relatively easy to avoid the problems of ani-

mating a movement too quickly. What is less easy to avoid is the opposite problem of overcompensating and going too slowly. It is easy to find yourself tempted into doing very slow animation, partly in an attempt to avoid going too quickly and partly because there can be something satisfying about the smooth, stately animation which results from doing things too slowly. Doing things slowly will indeed look pleasingly smooth, but it will also make your animation look weightless and floaty, as if it were taking place in space or underwater.

It is well advisable not to animate things too slowly, because, as well as making your film less interesting to watch, in most forms of animation it will mean that you have to

Although the gaps between these drawings might be small enough for the eye to bridge, there is not enough time for the brain to understand what it is seeing. If these drawings were on twos, then the fish would be in shot for only four frames (a sixth of a second) before disappearing.

This punch should be a quick and snappy movement – taking seven drawings to animate it will make it appear too slow and 'floaty'.

do much more work. It is interesting that computer animation seems particularly prone to floatiness; this is the only form of animation where slower animation does not involve more work since the computer generates the in-between images.

Getting things just right Getting the timing of movements right is partly a matter of experience. However, all animators can help themselves by acting out the moves they are animating. Although this feels odd to start with, it will really help to improve your animation. You may not be able to time exactly how many frames a move will take, but you will be able to get a very good idea. With longer scenes it is worth thinking about what they would look like if they formed a live action film; would they appear lifelike, or would they be in painstaking, slow motion? Of course, animation should exaggerate or distort real life, not

Varying the length of time taken over the moves between these poses will make the animation seem more lifelike.

reflect it accurately. However, it is much easier to do this if you study the real life movement you are exaggerating.

It is also important to vary the timing of different movements. For example, you might be animating a character sitting down at a table, picking his fork up and then reaching for the salt.

Although it is perfectly possible that each of these moves might take twelve frames, if you give all the moves this timing then the whole animation will appear robotic. Real people and animals tend not to move in such an even way. It would be better to take more time over the sitting down movement – say, twenty frames – then, after a short hold, have the character pick up the cutlery quickly, over just five frames, and, after another hold, have him make a speedy, impatient reach for the salt.

Timing of Holds

A hold is any part of your film where the camera rests on a character or background. It can be difficult to work out how long to keep holds on since there is no movement to act out. Because of this, the temptation is to keep them on for quite a short time and get on with the animation. This may make your film frantic – all movement, with no pauses. Admittedly much animation is like this, particularly when it comes to short films, think of the manic energy and movement which is almost constant in a Daffy Duck cartoon. However, you can achieve very different effects by letting the camera rest on still images. The films of Hayao Miyasaki, most famous for *Spirited Away*, creates a contemplative feel with holds or slow camera moves on landscapes or buildings.

A general rule to help you with holds is that an image needs to be on screen for at least eight frames, or a third of a second, to be registered by the viewer. This rule can be used when showing writing on-screen; allowing eight frames for every word on-screen will give you a good idea of how long to hold. In fact, that will often seem too long a hold, but it is better to leave it too long and guarantee that absolutely everyone has time to read it than to cut it short and have some viewers miss the joke or the information being communicated.

Dramatic Timing

Timing may be used in many different ways to create dramatic and comic effect. The most important factor is to allow time for the situation or joke to register with your audience. The memorable shorts from the golden age of animation have countless wonderful examples of dramatic timing. Think of the long, drawn out way in which Wile E. Coyote falls off a cliff – as soon as he steps off the cliff, the audience knows that he is doomed, but the moment is stretched out as he walks slowly into space, stops, looks down, looks back at the audience, horrified and then finally plummets. Tex Avery's *Droopy* cartoons are superb examples of varying the timing to keep things lively. More often than not, Droopy is still to the point of being comatose, but, once or twice in every episode, he goes absolutely insane, leaping around the screen or thumping himself round the head with excitement. These are just two examples, but every great piece of animation will contain good timing since this is the one thing that animation cannot do without.

MOVEMENT

The most important aspect about movement in animation is that it is clear. It is vital that your audience understand what your characters are doing, otherwise they will

Ones and Twos: How Many Frames to Use per Image?

We know that the trick of animation works by showing still images in quick succession to create a sense of movement. But exactly how quickly do these images have to be shown? It is possible to animate by creating a new image for every single frame in your film. This is called animating on ones, as each image is on for one frame. Animating on ones, or singles, as they are sometimes called, will result in very smooth animation but it will also require a lot of work. For this reason, much animation is animated on twos, with each image held for two frames instead of one. The time between the images is still small enough to create the illusion of movement, but you need to do only half the amount of work.

If you can animate perfectly well on twos, then why is some animation still done on singles? One reason is that animation for the cinema needs to be smoother than animation for television or the internet. Animation works by tricking your eye into bridging the gaps between successive drawings. On an average television, the gap might be only a small fraction of an inch; on a large cinema screen it could be as much as a foot. Doing cinema animation on ones makes the gaps between images much smaller since there are twice as many drawings for each movement. Of course, it helps that the budgets for feature films tend to be much bigger than those for television series, meaning that their makers can afford the luxury of animating on ones.

The second reason for animating on ones is that some movements are too quick to animate on twos. If you are animating a character thumping a desk, then the entire move might only take three frames. If animated on twos you would have only two images: one for the start of the move and one for the end. Animating on singles would allow you to have an in-between image.

Most television animation mixes up twos and ones. The bulk of the animation is done on twos, but any quick movements are done on ones, along with any effects, such as smoke or splashes, which need to be presented as smoothly as possible.

It is rarely a good idea to keep images which are part of a movement on screen for more than two frames. There are some exceptions to this; it is possible to do some well-stylized walk-cycles with each image on for three frames, but, in general, anything more than two frames per image causes the illusion of animation to break down. If you have animated something too quickly it may be tempting to put each image on for four frames instead of two to slow it down. However, this will result only in jerky animation; to successfully make it slower, you will need more images.

Animating this move on singles means that the move can be snappy and clear.

This drawing would make a good key since it is at the start of a movement.

This drawing is at the end of a move and so is another good key.

This drawing is in the middle of the move, which is not the right place for a key.

begin to switch off. Animation is always a stylized or exaggerated version of real life; this means that the movements made by humans and animals in real life may not appear clear when replicated by stylized cartoon characters. Whereas the design of animated characters may be more out-landish and unusual than is likely in real life, the movement made by those characters needs to be simpler and clearer than reality if it is to be understood.

The Importance Of Good Keys
The best way of ensuring that your charac-

ters' movements are clear is to take plenty of time and care over your key images. The clearer and simpler these are, the more readable your animation will be. When working at MGM, Tex Avery would often spend a couple of days creating the perfect key drawing; this meant that even the most frantic action scenes would be easy to read.

Where should keys go? Key images should represent the key part of a movement. This means that they should appear at the most extreme part of a movement – the begin-ning or the end – and not in the middle.

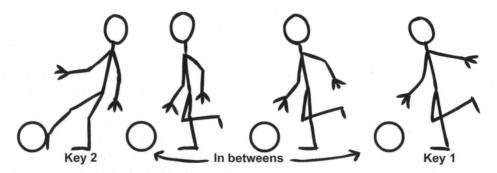

Key 2   ⟵ ___ In betweens ___ ⟶   Key 1

This set of drawings has two keys at the beginning and the end of the move and so any timing is possible. The in-betweens are positioned so that the move starts slowly and accelerates.

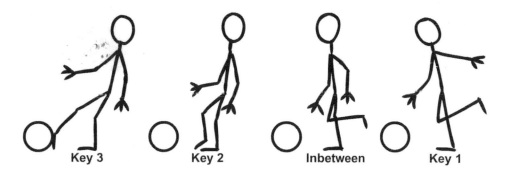

Key 3   Key 2   Inbetween   Key 1

This set of drawings has three keys, with one placed wrongly just past the middle of the move; this means that it is not possible for the move to accelerate as much as it should.

This drawing shows a man catching a ball, but is not particularly interesting.

This version is more exaggerated and more interesting as a result.

With animation, it is worth pushing exaggeration as far as possible.

Keys are designed to make the task of animating easier since they allow you to plan where your movement is going before you animate it. By playing with the timing between keys you can see how a move could look with different timings. Placing keys in the wrong part of the movement actually limits the amount of playing around that you can do since it will dictate some of the timing of your move before you have even begun to do in-betweens.

What should keys look like? Keys appear at the extreme points of a movement, as we have seen, and so it is important that they look like extremes. Do not be cautious with your key images, but make them as exaggerated as possible.

The other important point about key drawings is to make sure that they form a good silhouette (*see* Chapter 5). Creating animation that is readable in silhouette is a good way of making sure that your film will be clearly understandable. Of course, if you are doing model or stop-motion animation you will not be able to use key images. However, you can apply the same principles to the drawings you make for

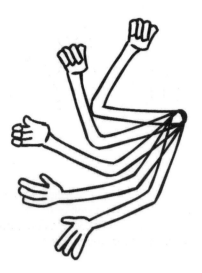

All the images in this animation are evenly spaced. This means that the movement will progress at an even speed, neither speeding up nor slowing down.

your storyboard and it is just as important to include clearly readable positions in your animation.

Getting In-betweens Right

Once you have created some distinctive keys at the extreme points of movement it may be hard to know how to space the rest of your images out. The temptation can be to put an even amount of space between every single image. Although this is the easiest way of animating, it will lead to your animation looking robotic, with every action moving at an even rate. It is much better to vary the space between your in-between images so that movements happen at differing speeds.

The smaller the distance between images, the slower the move will appear. By starting a move with the images very close together and then gradually increasing the distance between them, you can show

By concentrating the in-between images at the beginning of the animation, the movement starts slowly and gets quicker.

By making the distance between images smaller towards the end, the movement slows down.

acceleration. It is also possible to do the reverse, to have a movement become slower towards its end. This is sometimes referred to as 'cushioning a movement'.

Animators often use both acceleration and cushioning in the same movement. If you are animating someone jumping, he will start slowly and then accelerate into the air. He will slow down as he gets to the peak of his jump as he loses the energy gained from the push off; finally he will accelerate as gravity takes hold and he falls to the ground.

This jump includes both the acceleration and the cushioning of movement.

Move in Arcs

Most natural movement occurs not in straight lines but in arcs. The way our arms and legs are pivoted around joints means that they move along a smooth, curved path; try bending your own arm and looking at the shape it creates.

Because arcs are the natural shape of human and animal movement, they are also the most natural shape to watch. The

eye expects to see this kind of movement, so when it sees straight or jerky animation instead your audience will instinctively know that something is wrong, even if they cannot tell what it is. Keeping your characters moving in arcs has much to do with keeping them on model. An arm or a leg

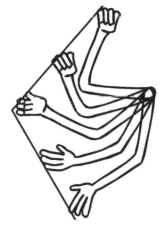

This arm movement moves in a straight line ...

This movement moves jerkily...

This arm moves in an arc, which is both realistic and easy to look at.

One of the arms in this animation is too long and so the arc movement is broken.

naturally swings in an arc and so if your animation does not then it is most likely to be because the length of the limb has changed.

Making Movement Visible

It is surprising how often an audience fails to read or even see an animated move. This is not necessarily because it is not paying attention, but because it was not expecting the move to happen. There may be more than one character on screen, as well as background elements and effects animation – do not assume that your audience will automatically look at the right place at the right time. If a movement takes you by surprise then, by the time you see it properly, it is already halfway through. How do you let

By adding an anticipation movement to this animation you are letting your audience know that the character is about to jump. This means that the jump will appear clearer.

By moving the hand back into a pose of anticipation before it grabs the cake, the animation is much clearer.

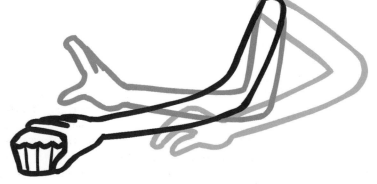

The overshoot in this animation will give the punch some bounce at the end, making it more lifelike.

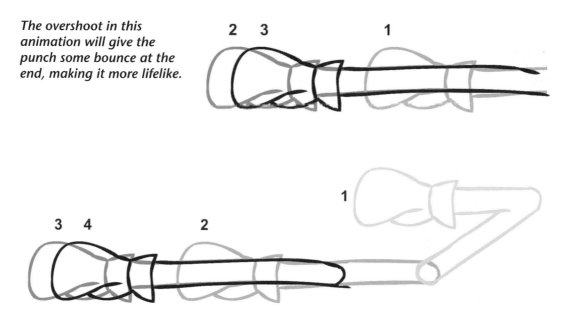

With anticipation and overshoot this simple punch animation will have real life to it.

your audience know that something is going to happen? The best way is to use something called anticipation.

Anticipation Every big movement is preceded by a smaller one in the opposite direction. For instance, before jumping up into the air, you bend your knees down, and before kicking a football forwards, you move your foot backwards. In animation these smaller movements are referred to as 'anticipation', and a good use of it will greatly help your animation.

Anticipation may be used in many kinds of movement, from the big to the small. It works well on a jump, a kick or a punch, but it is just as useful when animating much smaller moves.

Overshoot Overshoot is to the end of a movement what anticipation is to the beginning. It makes a move more lifelike

and much easier to watch. Human movement rarely, if ever, comes to an abrupt stop. It is much more likely to slow down into a gradual stop – cushioning – or, in the case of faster moves, go slightly beyond its ending point before coming back to rest. This second movement is called 'overshoot'.

By using anticipation at the beginning of a move and overshoot at the end you can give your animation a real sense of life. But, although anticipation can be used in almost every situation, overshoot really works only with quicker moves. It is better to use cushioning for slower moves since using overshoot on them will make them appear jerky.

Keeping things simple Keeping your movement as simple as possible is one of the best ways of making it appear clear to your audience. It will also make it easier to animate. In part, keeping things simple is about leaving out superfluous animation. For instance, if you are animating a character queuing up to buy an ice cream you could show him shuffling along the queue, turning to look at the price list of ice creams, then shuffling along some more before turning again to order. However, this means animating a lot of action that is not vital to the story; it will take up much time and it will also make your animation unclear since you will be surrounding the important movement with other animation. It would be much clearer and easier to show the character in the queue, then cut to the price list and then to the character ordering an ice cream. This conveys the same information as before but is clearer and much easier to animate.

Always be on the lookout for unnecessary movement in your film, and be prepared to move and cheat to make things easier, if need be. If your character has to press a button on his desk, and the button is too far away for him to reach, instead of animating your character getting up and walking over to the button, why not just move the button? If you want your audience to concentrate on your film, then you want to make sure that it is not full of unnecessary movement.

The other good way of keeping things simple is to break complicated movements into separate, smaller ones. If you were animating a character leaping up from her chair to cling on to a light bulb before sliding along the tabletop, you could attempt to animate it as one movement, using just two keys at the beginning and the end. However, that is a hard way of doing things, and it may make your animation look unnatural. It would be much better and easier to break such moves into a series of smaller ones, each marked with a set of key drawings.

Lip Sync

More than almost any other area of animation, lip sync is about creating something that works rather than something entirely realistic and accurate. This is because, when lip sync is successful, no one notices it, since the viewers are too busy watching the film. It is only when the lip sync goes badly wrong that it catches the eye.

Getting started To animate lip sync, you first need to make sure that you have a breakdown of the voice track to your film (*see* Chapter 6 for details on how to do this). The next thing to do is to work out which are the important sounds in the piece to get right. The important sounds occur where the mouth is firmly shut (the sounds associated with *b*, *p*, *m*, *f* and *v*) and

This move is broken into smaller moves to make it easier to animate successfully.

also with long vowel sounds. Lip sync works much better if it is animated straightahead – this gives it a nice flow and continuity – so do not use these important sounds as keys, just keep them in mind as you begin animating.

Animating lip-sync When you begin animating your lip synch straightahead, it is better to go straight into big, open mouth shapes and then animate more gradually out of them. If you animate both in and out of an open mouth shape your character will appear as loose lipped, as if he had too much to drink. When it comes to hitting those important mouth shut sounds, always make sure that they are on for two frames, and preferably for three or even four. If the sound they are representing is actually only a frame long, have the mouth shut image appear a couple of frames earlier, cutting off the end of the previous word, otherwise it will not be properly visible.

Avoid shutting the mouth too often; most people are quite lazy with their mouth when they are talking and leave their mouth slightly open between sentences, rather than shutting it tightly. Try to reflect this in your animation, otherwise your lip synch will appear too busy and will distract the audience from the main animation.

Furthermore, when animating a very fast piece of dialogue you may need to cut out parts of words or even entire words to get it to work properly; if you try to animate every single word you will again fall into the trap of your lip synch being too busy.

It is worth keeping lip sync in mind when designing your characters' mouths. You need to decide whether their mouths will show both the upper and the lower teeth when they are open, only the upper teeth and the tongue, just the tongue or even nothing apart from a dark shape. Any of these options is acceptable, but it is important to be consistent when animating them. For instance, if you are going to show teeth in your animation, make sure that you show them in as many mouth shapes as possible. If teeth appear in only a third of your lip synch animation, then they will look like a white light, flashing on and off in the middle of your character's face.

Some claim that lip synch works best when it is actually slightly out of sync. That is, by moving the animation so that mouth shapes appear two or three frames before the sound that they represent. This makes it trickier to animate and does not always have the desired effect. The best thing to do is to animate the lip synch in synch, and, if it does not look quite right, then try

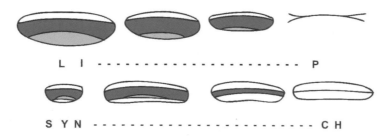

The shut mouth for the p of lip starts slightly earlier to make sure that it is on screen for long enough. Also notice how the big, open mouth shapes come up straightaway and that the phrase finishes on a slightly open mouth.

These lines can give a greater impression of speed.

Dry brush lines could blur an entire character in a fast move.

All these extra legs will give the impression of chaotic, frantic movement.

moving the sound forward a few frames in postproduction.

Tricks

Animators use all manner of curious and unrealistic devices to help their animation look better. These devices are sometimes referred to as tricks, because when they work well the eye does not even know that they are there. As soon as a trick becomes obvious to the audience, it more often than not stops working. The use of the following tricks can help your animation appear sharper and snappier, but they must be used sparingly. If you get carried away with tricks and start to use them all the time, the audience will start to notice them and they will no longer work.

Whiz lines When an object or a character is moving quickly you can enhance the feeling of speed by showing lines streaming out behind it. Whiz lines are more often found in comic books, where they are necessary to indicate movement in still images. However, they are often used in animation, particularly to enhance cartoony, unrealistic animation – *Scooby Doo* is a good example; Shaggy and Scooby always leave the screen in a puff of dust and a trail of whiz lines.

In the days when animation was painted on cel, whiz lines were often done by using a dry brush with paint, creating a scratchy but flowing line which would sometimes obscure almost the whole character. Dry brushwork was used to great effect in Tex Avery's films, as well as cropping up all the time in the frantic action of the *Roadrunner* cartoons. Whiz lines and dry brushes should be used only for a few frames at a time – put them on screen for too long, and it will look as if your characters are being chased by flying snakes or morphing into blurred images of themselves.

This animation will not really work: the gap between the images is too big and so the animation will flicker or strobe.

This smeared in-between will make the move work without having to slow it down.

Extra limbs To create the impression of a character moving frantically, you can give him many more arms and legs than he would actually have. This is another technique which frequently appeared in *Roadrunner*, as well as being used to great effect in the classic Canadian short film *The Cat Came Back*. When using extra limbs like this, it is best to have them appear at random. If you try to animate them properly, then it will look as if your character had actually grown an extra five legs.

Smears It is possible to stretch or smear in-between images to allow you to make a movement between keys even quicker.

Using smeared in-betweens will create very quick, slick animation, and, like many of these tricks, it was first mastered by Tex

Avery; it also appears frequently in the television series *Johnny Bravo*. As with most such tricks, smearing only works when used on quick moves. It is best to make sure that smeared images are on screen for only a single frame at a time, otherwise the viewer will notice your character stretch and distort.

Squash and stretch As well as smearing, it is possible to distort your characters in other ways to enhance their movements – making them stretch when reaching or jumping, and squash when flinching or hiding. Squash and stretch really took off with the *Looney Tunes* films and has been used (and often overused) ever since.

Squash and stretch will not work for every kind of animation or every type of

95

This character (left) can be distorted: either squashed (below left), or stretched (below right).

character. The Warner Brothers characters, with their simple, bean-like bodies were ideally suited to it; other, more detailed or realistic characters are not. It is easy to get carried away and to overuse it, with the end result that everyone and everything in your film appears to be made of rubber.

ACTING

Whereas movement is all about the technical side of animation – thinking about the precise details of time and distance – acting has much more to do with creativity. It can be just as hard to get right as movement, and in many ways is actually even harder.

For instance, if you are animating a man jumping in the air, you know where he is starting his jump and where he is finishing and you can plan the move accordingly. Animating the same man moving from the depths of despair to a sudden look of quiet hopefulness is far less precise. However, there are a number of ways of making acting easier for yourself and clearer for your audience.

How to Make Your Acting Clear
Think big It would be more accurate to call this section 'overacting', because with animation exaggeration and over-the-top acting work far better than minimalism.

This pose shows despair in an understated way.

This overacted pose would work much better.

Think of how a character like Daffy Duck acts: he bounces around the screen with excitement one minute, sobs and staggers with despair the next, then rubs his hands with glee at a cunning plan. In reality, nobody behaves anything like this. Even in live action drama such behaviour is seen only in deliberately hammy and exaggerated performances, such as pantomime. But in animation it works, and is much clearer to watch than more realistic, toned down acting.

Keep your emotions separate In real life we can often express several emotions at one time. If you are taking your girlfriend to meet your family for the first time, you might find yourself trying to feign interest in your dad's tedious story while at the same time trying to get your mum's attention so that she can shut him up. While doing these, you could also be beginning to cringe with embarrassment and seethe with rage. Such a complex combination of emotions would be almost impossible to communicate clearly in animation. It would be much better to separate the emotions out and show them one after another.

Showing these emotions separately makes them easier to animate and watch.

The Simpsons provides a good example of how to express emotions. Characters change their expressions quickly, hold one so that it can be seen and understood, then switch to another.

How to Keep Your Characters Alive

One of the biggest problems with animation is how to stop your characters appearing to revert into inanimate objects as soon as they have finished talking or doing something. This often happens with characters when they are not the main focus of the scene but are supposed to be listening to another character or watching something happen. Of course, you could just keep the characters moving all the time to avoid this problem, but this involves much extra work and can also distract your audience from the main focus of the scene. But if you keep them completely still they may look like they have been switched off. So how do you keep your characters looking alive?

The importance of eyelines One of the main reasons for characters appearing to be switched off is that their eyes seem to glaze over. This happens when an observing character apparently fails to respond to a changing action or the movement of another character by always looking in the same direction. This results in your character's appearing to be in a trance. By making sure that his eyes are always looking in the right direction, towards the focus of the scene, you can make your animation look much more lively.

Moving holds Another way of using eyes to keep a character looking lively is to have him blink once in a while. On average, people blink once every three or four seconds, and your characters will seem more alive if

they do this too. It may not sound much, but it can make a real difference.

Keeping a character entirely still apart from an occasional blink is often referred to as a 'moving hold' since the character's pose is held, but is given just enough movement to keep him looking alive. You do not necessarily have to use a blink as the movement in a moving hold; any small movement, such as tapping a foot, drumming fingers or biting fingernails will do. Moving holds are intended to save you time, so it is best if the movement does not require a great deal of animation. Moving holds are a quick way of keeping your film looking lively all the way through without having to spend time producing detailed animation for every single scene.

EFFECTS

In animation, effects refer to any animation not dealing with characters or solid objects. They include weather, shadows, lightning, explosions and water. Effects animation is not subject to the same practical rules as character animation; it can be highly stylized, unrealistic and even random and still work. It is often a matter of doing what looks best, rather than struggling to produce something that looks realistic.

Water

Water is particularly hard to animate, mainly because it can change so quickly. It can bubble, splash, froth, drip and gush, all in one movement. To animate water successfully you often need to simplify and stylize it, turning it into simpler shapes and colours. We are so used to seeing this stylizing that it often does not even register. For example, in real life the sea is usually a murky, dark green colour, but in most cartoons it is a flat blue.

Drips and splashes These can be hard work to animate because they have a habit of multiplying. You might begin animating a single drip, but once that splashes on to the ground it will split into lots of smaller drips.

This problem of multiplying drips is even bigger with splashes. For this reason animators often stylize splashes, animating them to appear and disappear quite quickly.

Rivers and seas When animating large areas of water it becomes even more important to stylize the animation. Unless you have the time and the budget to spend on the realistic water effects seen in films such as *The Perfect Storm*, stylizing the water will be the only way of doing things. A good way of animating rivers is to concentrate on animating the reflections on the surface or even floating leaves or other objects. This will convey the river's movement without

This drip divides into eight smaller drips when it splashes.

This splash reaches full size almost instantly, before quickly breaking up into smaller drips. These smaller ones can be made to disappear quickly, without it looking as if the splash had been turned off.

In this wave cycle one wave animates so that it turns into the next, and so on. This will create simple, cartoony sea animation.

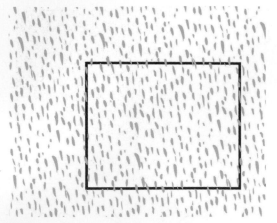

Moving this large, still image of rain across the screen will create a rainstorm.

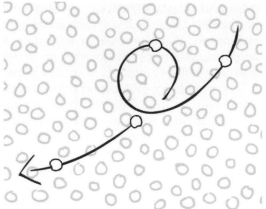

Snowflakes can drift and spiral, instead of falling straight down.

your having to get involved in complex water animation. As for animating the sea, it is best to use a simple, stylized wave cycle to create the right kind of movement.

An even simpler way of animating the sea is to leave it as a flat, still shape and show wave movement by the way you animate the movement of boats and fish in the sea.

Weather

Changing the weather in your film can help to create an entirely different atmosphere, and it can be done fairly easily.

Rain Rain can be animated quite simply: create a huge image of a rainy sky, then move it down and across the screen to create a rainstorm. To prevent this from looking too artificial, you can create another layer of rain effects, showing a few drops falling and splashing on the ground closer to the camera.

Snow Snow can be animated in a similar fashion to rain: create a large image of a snowstorm, then move it across the screen.

As with the rain, include a few snowflakes nearer the front of the screen to prevent it from looking too artificial. These flakes should float and drift, rather than fall straight down.

Mist and fog The important point with mist and fog is to make sure that they never stay still, but move as slowly as possible. If they move too quickly, they will look more like smoke; if they stay still, they could start to look more like a solid object. Fog should hang in the air and drift about slowly, with no particular sense of purpose or direction.

Lightning and electricity When electricity moves through the air, as happens with lightning or the kind of electric shocks which frequently appear at the slapstick end of animation, it is trying to get from one point to another as quickly as possible. When animating electricity you can have its shape change at random as long as you make sure that it stays attached at these two points.

100

The start and the end of the bolt of lightning stay in the same place, but every other part of it moves at random. Adding a negative image to the bolt will create a flash.

Explosions

Explosions, thankfully, appear much more often in cartoons than they do in real life. The best way of animating them is to have them fill the screen immediately and then have them gradually fade out.

The explosion itself can be stylized in several different ways.

Fire

If you try to animate fire as a conventional shape it does not really work – you end with something that looks like a ragged, orange blanket blowing in the breeze. It works far better if you animate it as different, unrelated shapes appearing at random; this creates the flickering effect of flames. By combining this random flickering with more conventionally animated offshoots of flame you can create quite a good effect.

Smoke

The animation of smoke is prone to the same problems as in animating water: you begin animating one shape but end by having to animate tens, even hundreds. Smoke (and for that matter steam) will always dissolve into the surrounding air, which means that it will break up into smaller elements before disappearing completely.

Smoke also has a distinctive way of moving, wobbling and swaying from side to side (this is called Brownian motion, the result of molecular bombardment by

Bringing this explosion up instantly will be much more dramatic than making it appear gradually.

You could stylize your
explosion like this ...

... or like this.

*The combination of randomly cycled images of the main flame with animated offshoots
creates a convincing fire.*

atmospheric gases). To include all this in your animation you will need to stylize your smoke.

Shadows

Giving your animation shadows can involve much more work than you might expect. Unless you are working in model or 3D animation you will have to animate a shadow for every single move your character makes. In other forms of animation, particularly drawn animation, this can mean creating a separate image of a shadow for every single character drawing you have done; in short, using shadows, along with the tones and rims that go with them, could almost double the amount of work you have to do.

Because of this amount of work, drawn animation has traditionally stayed away from shadows. However, since *Who Framed Roger Rabbit?*, which used shadows to give the animation the feel of film noir, as well as helping it fit in with the live action, there has been a much greater interest in

To animate smoke, you have to stylize it to some degree.

using shadows. *Space Jam*, another film combining animation with live action, had several animators working solely on shadows (even though the *Looney Tunes* characters featured in the film were originally

You could animate this character without shadows ...

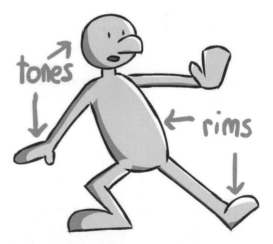

... but adding rims and tones to the character will make it appear less flat, although it will take a long time.

103

animated with no shadows at all). It is important to remember that the use of shadows is as much an economic decision as an artistic one. Once you start to give characters rims and tones you will need to make sure that they have them throughout the film for the sake of continuity, so do not start drawing shadows until you are certain you have the time and the money to finish them off.

LIMITED ANIMATION

Although this chapter has tried to demonstrate all the things you can do with your animation in an ideal world, you are obviously unlikely to have this luxury when making your own film. You will inevitably be short of time and money when working on your film and will need to do your best with the resources at hand. To do this, you will often need to make use of limited animation.

Limited animation is the name given to the set of skills developed by animators over the years to make the most of tight budgets. By simplifying your animation as much as possible and by using a variety of tricks with camera work, backgrounds, storyboards and animation, it is possible to tell any story with any budget. The art of telling the grandest stories with only limited resources is almost as creative, and certainly as useful, as the skills required to be a top animator. Limited animation is invaluable to anyone making his or her own film, but the techniques have been used in many television series (*Roobarb and Custard* is a classic example; *South Park* a more recent one).

Lip-synch
Lip-synch can be one of the most labour-intensive parts of film-making. Even small, simple films will often have a large amount of dialogue in them. If that dialogue is being lip-synched it must be done accurately to avoid distracting the audience. There are ways of dealing with lip-synch in limited animation. The first is simply to avoid it wherever possible. The best example of this is *Dangermouse*, which would always open with a sequence featuring the hero talking to his boss, Colonel K, on a video link. The animation would focus on the listener instead of the speaker, meaning that the entire sequence could be animated without having to do any lip-synch. This idea could be used in several ways. If characters are talking in an office, you could show them as silhouettes viewed through a window, or even show just a shot of the outside of the office door. If characters are outside, show them in long shot, so that they are tiny, lip-synch-free figures on the horizon.

Of course, no matter how cleverly you use such tricks you will sometimes still need to animate a piece of lip-synch. However, this can be done relatively quickly by simplifying the mouth shapes you use. It is possible to do limited but watchable lip-synch with just five mouth shapes: an *aah* sound, an *ee* sound and an *oo* sound, along with a closed mouth and a shape for *f*.

Camera Work
Camera work in limited animation is used to make as much as possible of the scenes you create. A slow pan across a background will keep things moving and distract your audience from realizing that they are looking at a still, unanimated image. Any of the devices used in lip-synch – showing characters in silhouette, focusing on an office door while characters talk inside – will often work better with a camera move.

Good Ideas

As you get the hang of limited animation, you will start to spot ideas which are ideally suited to it. These need not be small or cautious ideas, just ones that will be easy to animate. Any animation taking place in a snow-covered wilderness – a search for the yeti, Scott's journey to the South Pole – could be done very easily since the background need be nothing more complicated than a blank sheet of paper. Animation taking place in the sea or the sky can be equally light on backgrounds. For example, look at the Hanna-Barbera series *Dastardly and Mutley in their Flying Machine* (sometimes known as *Stop the Pigeon*). Nearly all the animation takes place in the sky, with only a plain blue background required. Do not be afraid to use any idea which may save time, however corny it may seem: characters walking into a cave or basement, where only their eyes are visible, can save a huge amount of time.

If there is no time to animate something, then just cut straight to the end of the movement. Provided that your key positions are clear enough and your timing is good, you can get away with using few or even no in-betweens. Bob Godfrey's *Henry's Cat* is an excellent example of how far this technique, combined with good ideas and a funny script, can take you.

Recycle

Another good way of getting the most out of limited animation is to reuse your animation wherever possible. If your character is playing ten pin bowls there is no need to do a new piece of animation for every ball he bowls. It is far better to spend a little more time on a single piece of animation and then reuse it. Always keep an eye out for any opportunities to reuse animation in

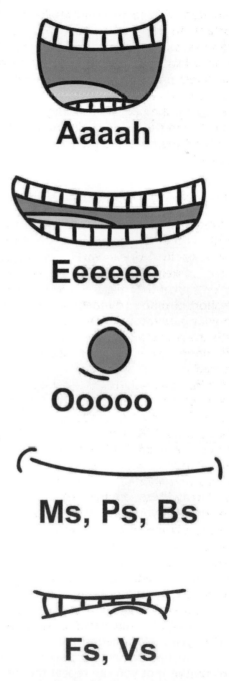

Aaaah

Eeeeee

Ooooo

Ms, Ps, Bs

Fs, Vs

You can do limited but successful lip-synch using just five mouth shapes.

If your story happens to include some dark spaces, you could make some scenes very quick to animate.

your film; these do not have to be big movements, you could cut back to the same reaction shot of a character more than once in a conversation.

As well as reusing separate pieces of animation you could loop pieces of it, making the last image lead straight into the first of the repeated animation to create a continuous cycle. The most commonly used example of cycles in animation are walk cycles. Once you have animated two steps of a walk on the spot you can repeat these steps while scrolling a background image backwards behind it. By using this method it is

possible to animate a character walking through an entire forest or a city with only a couple of seconds of actual animation.

Walk cycles are found in all areas of animation, but probably nowhere more famously than in the *Scooby Doo* series. These would often feature characters walking or running down shadowy corridors for improbably long periods of time, often passing the same door more than once as even the background scrolling behind them was looped.

Using cycles and repeating animation is probably the easiest of limited animation

This walk cycle may be repeated to make the character walk for as long as you want.

tricks for an audience to spot. For this reason it is important to use them carefully. Limited animation is at its most successful when you are not aware of it.

Consistency

The most important thing about limited animation is to use it consistently. Limited animation works best when the audience do not notice the limitations and can concentrate on enjoying the film. If this is to happen, you need to make sure that you do not draw any unnecessary attention to the devices and short cuts you have used. For example, if you find yourself with some spare time at the end of the schedule, it may be tempting to go back to the climactic scene of the film and re-lip-synch it in a more sophisticated style, as well as adding some background animation of trees blowing in the wind. You might reasonably expect this to improve your film, but your extra work will actually have quite the opposite effect. One scene of more complex animation will highlight the limitations elsewhere, drawing your audience's attention to them and distracting them from the film itself.

8 POST-PRODUCTION

This section of the book covers everything you need to do once you have finished animating your film. This includes adding sound effects and any additional visual effects, and, most importantly, turning the film into a finished version which people will be able to watch. In this chapter we shall look at the different skills and equipment you can use to make the finished film look and sound as good as possible.

SOUND EFFECTS

Although the voice track for your film needs to be recorded before you begin the animation, sound effects and incidental music are always added at the post-production stage. This is because you cannot tell what an action will sound like until it is been animated. There are many different ways of animating a piano fall on someone's head, for instance – it could splinter into a thousand pieces, it could remain intact and flatten its victim to a pancake or it could crash straight through the floor, each of these will need its distinctive sound effects.

Matching your animation with the right sound effect will improve both the sound and the look of your film, so it is important to get it right and wait till the animation is complete.

This will have a solid, heavy sound effect.

This will need a chaotic, splintering sound.

Where Can You Find Sound Effects?

Finding sound effects for your film is not as complicated as you might feel. Searching the internet for free sound effect downloads or something similar will produce thousands of sites offering sound effects to download. Even sites where you have to pay for sound effects will often be asking for only a couple of dollars for an effect. Some companies sell CDs featuring a range of sounds on a particular theme. This may be useful if your film is set in a very noisy environment, such as a rainforest or a factory; a CD full of different jungle effects will save you from having to reuse the same clip of chirruping frogs throughout your film, sending your audience and yourself mad. Making use of downloadable sounds and the occasional effects CD means that, with patience, it is possible to pick up almost all of the sounds you need for very little money.

Of course, some effects may be almost impossible to find and so you have to resort to making them for yourself. Most computers come with basic sound recording equipment, and a simple microphone can be bought from most computer shops for very little. It is then simply a matter of keeping the room as quiet as possible, staying close to the microphone and producing your sound effect, whatever it may be.

Obviously, home-recorded effects may not sound as clear as professionally recorded ones will. It is always important to have good sound quality, but when it comes to sound effects you can sometimes get away with a lower sound quality than you can with voice-overs. Because a sound effect will often appear once only in a film, the audience are less likely to pick up on the sound quality. Also, from a practical point of view, it is not very cost-effective to hire a recording studio to make a single sound effect.

You can avoid some of the problems involved in creating your own sound effects by not being too literal-minded with your requirements. If you are animating a balloon filled with porridge exploding, a generic, cartoony, squelchy sound will most likely be more effective, and certainly less messy, than filling a real balloon with porridge and holding a microphone next to it while you burst it.

How To Use Sound Effects

You can use sound effects in a variety of different ways. The traditionally, cartoony way is to use effects wherever possible – whenever characters blink, move, break into a run or screech to a halt, then a sound effect plays. With this style of sound effect, it is more important for the effect to sound funny than accurate. For instance, siren noises may be used to soundtrack a shocked double take, or hectic xylophone music to soundtrack a run-cycle. This is the way sound effects were used in much of the Golden Age of animation, from the early Disney films to *Looney Tunes*.

The opposite of this is to go for more realistic, toned-down effects. This means using believable sound effects only, and leaving sound effects off any movement which would be silent in real life, such as blinks. This style of using sound effects is common in more realistic, adult animation, such as *King of the Hill*.

In between these extremes lie many variations, and it is up to you to find the one which is right for your film. What is important is to be consistent in your use of sound effects: if your character's feet make a squeaking noise when he walks in the first scene of your film, you need to make sure you maintain that effect throughout the film; if that is too annoying, then take the sound effect off every walk. If sound effects appear on some scenes but not others they will only distract and confuse the audience.

Music

Music can add a huge amount to your film, transforming the mood of scenes and creating an atmosphere. However, as with images, you need to make sure that you have the legal right to use the music. Recorded sound stays in copyright for fifty years after it was originally recorded; after that, it may be used by anyone.

It is possible to use music before its fifty-year spell of copyright is up, but you need to make sure that the music is licensed. This means contacting the people who own the copyright of the recording (usually, but not always, the record company) and getting them to give you licence to use it. There is no limit to how much it could cost to

This animation will need the noise of splintering floorboards as well as piano sounds.

license a piece of music: it could be less than £100, but sometimes it could cost hundreds of thousands of pounds. As a general guide, consider the following points, all of which will have some effect on how much it could cost to license a piece of music:

- The piece of music itself: the Rolling Stones will be more expensive than St. Winifred's School choir.
- The medium in which you will be using it: licensing music for the internet will be cheaper than doing so for a feature film.
- How it will appear in your film: to use the music as incidental backing will be cheaper than using it for the title sequence; if you are using a song for both the opening titles and the end credits and the name of the song as the film's title, it will be more expensive still.
- How long you want to use it for: you could license a track forever or for just the week of a film festival you are showing your film at.

There are a number of ways of making your use of music affordable. The first, already mentioned, is to use music which is already out of copyright. However, you need to make sure the recording is out of copyright, too, not just the music. The piece of music that is Beethoven's *Ode to Joy* is out of copyright, but a recording made of it last year will not be. This means you must either license that recording, find another recording which is out of copyright or record a new version of the piece yourself for free. This last option can be quite productive: a home recording of your little sister playing Beethoven on her recorder could have more charm than a recording by the London Symphony Orchestra, and it will certainly be cheaper.

Another option is to use what is called 'library music'. This is music created specifically for incidental use in films, television and radio. The downside of this is that it will not be at all well known, but the upside is that you will be able to license it for a fraction of the cost needed for famous songs. A quick internet search will reveal a good many library music companies, often selling CDs of themed music.

It is worth mentioning here the money-saving tricks which might be tempting, but will not be successful. One of these it to try to dodge licensing problems by only using a tiny part of a piece of music. This simply will not work: it does not matter how small the piece of music you are using is, using it without permission will still count as an infringement of copyright. Another even simpler and more tempting option is simply to do nothing at all, on the grounds that the chances of anyone finding out that you have used their music are too small to be worth worrying about. This course of action is not recommended. Of course, some common sense needs to be applied; if you are making an animated birthday card to email to your mother, it is not so vital that you license the recording of *Happy Birthday* used in the animation. However, if you are making a film which will be shown to the public, be it at a film festival, on the internet or even on television, it is very important to sort out the music licensing as soon as possible. If you do not, then you run the risk that the record company which owns the copyright will make an injunction to stop your film from being shown anywhere, to anyone.

If you are in any doubt about what to do about the music in your film, it is worth talking to one of the professional bodies which deals with music copyright. In Britain the Performing Rights Society (PRS) works to collect licence fees for all music broadcast. If you are recording a new version of a copyrighted piece of music, you might also need to talk to the Mechanical-Copyright Protection Society (MCPS), which acts on behalf of composers to make agreements for the recording of their music. In the USA the American Society of Composers, Authors and Publishers is the best point of call. All countries have some similar bodies, and most of them are represented globally by the International Confederation of Societies of Authors and Composers (CISAC). CISAC's website (www.cisac.org) is a good starting point if you want to find out the body representing composers in a particular country.

VISUAL EFFECTS

The last chapter dealt with the ways in which you can add effects to your film. However, some of the effects you may want to use need to be done in post-production, rather than in the main animating process. For example, you may have made

a science fiction film using drawn animation, but, to give your lasers a real space-age look, you want to create them in a computer visual effects program. Even less spectacular effects, such as snow and rain, traditionally drawn by specialist effects animators, are now often produced in post-production.

However, in general, it is best to animate as much as possible during the main stage of animating. This is partly because it will be easier to animate a scene in one go than return to it weeks or even months later and try to remember exactly what you wanted it to look like (although obviously your storyboard should help you with this). It is also because adding too many spectacular visual effects can result in their jarring with the rest of the film. A simple, stylized, drawn animation film might look better with drawn weather effects instead of elaborate, 3D-animated thunderstorms.

The visual effects stage of post-production does not have to involve any animation at all. Special effects can sometimes be about applying filters to your imported

Visual Effects Software

The two main visual effects packages are After Effects for the PC and Shake for Macs. Both packages will let you animate on top of your imported film in both 2D and 3D space, although Shake has the more sophisticated 3D animation options, allowing you to morph and warp images. However, this means that it is also the more expensive option. In early 2004 After Effects cost around $1,500 and Shake around twice that amount. It is worth noting that, as with most 3D animation packages, After Effects will not work with the versions of Windows found on many home computers; for example, it is compatible with Windows 2000, but not with Windows ME.

Adobe After Effects	Microsoft Windows 2000 or XP
	Intel Pentium III or 4 processor
Shake	Mac OS X v10.3.3 or later
	800MHz or faster PowerPC G4

footage to change the way the whole film looks. This could involve giving your animation the rough, grainy texture of old-fashioned film, or even just filtering bright colours to make them safe for television. Visual effects programs can also be the best way to do camera moves, particularly if you do not have much experience with a real camera.

PRODUCING YOUR FILM

Once you have all your sound effects and music in place you are ready to add it to your animation and voice recording and produce your finished film. How much work this involves depends greatly on two things: the kind of animation you have used and the way you want to show it. If you have created a simple, 2D, computer-animated film to show on the internet, your post-production could consist of little more than exporting the film as a Flash player or QuickTime file. In contrast, if you have made a model animation film to be shown on video, you will need more time and technology to get things right.

Producing Animation to Watch on Computer

Computers are a cheap and easy way for your animation to reach a wide audience. Most people have access to the internet at home or at work, and if your film is too big to download you can burn a CD or even a DVD. The main formats for viewing animation on computers are as follows:

- avi files are designed for Windows machines and can therefore be viewed by most Windows users, although it is also possible to watch them on Macs. When exporting computer animation files as an avi file, you can keep the file size small by reducing the size and the quality of the image. It is best to do this if you want people to download or email your film; however, if you are showing your film on a CD it is possible to keep the quality much higher.

- Flash player files or swf files are the format created for exporting animation from Flash, although other programs such as Toon Boom Studio can now export swfs; swfs may be viewed on both PCs and Macs which have Flash Player installed; most computers now come with this already installed as part of their internet browser. Because Flash was designed for the internet this format can produce very low file sizes. This works best with cut-out style animation incorporating simple artwork created in Flash – more fluid, drawn animation will produce much bigger files. Exporting as an swf gives you fewer parameters to adjust; whereas avis and QuickTime movies can be set up to suit different viewing formats or editing packages, there are no such options in Flash player, which is primarily designed for internet viewing.

- QuickTime movies, or mov files, were designed for use on Apple Macs, although they may also be watched on PCs which have QuickTime player. However, as a general rule, Macs are much more likely to be able to show QuickTimes and PCs are more likely to be able to show avi files, so try to use a format which will suit the people that you hope will be watching your film.

How you go about turning your animation into one of these formats depends on the kind of animation you are working with.

Computer animation All computer animation programs should allow you to export your animation as one of these formats relatively easily. They can then be burned on to a CD or a DVD, or uploaded on to a website for viewing. If you decide to show your film on a website, then you need to take the file size of the final film into account, along with the people you want to see it. If you want your film to be viewed by animation and television companies then the file size is less of a worry since they are likely to have high-speed internet connections. If it is designed to be watched by friends and family, or anyone with a slow dial-up connection, it is worth keeping the file size, and therefore the download time, as small as possible.

Video animation To convert animation shot on video so that it can be viewed on computers you will need a video editing program (see below for more information). You will also need a way of connecting your video camera to your computer to transfer the images into the program. The equipment you need to do this depends on the type of camera you have: if you have a digital video camera you can use a firewire cable and a firewire card installed in your computer; if you have a traditional analogue camera you will need an analogue-to-digital conversion device, which will be able to transform your analogue footage into digital images.

Once your video is inside the computer it will be easy to export it as an avi, QuickTime or swf file. It will also be possible to use a video editing program to add a variety of special effects to the film (*see* Chapter 7 for more details).

Producing Animation to Watch on Video

If you want people to be able to watch your animation on video then you need to make use of a video editing package. This will allow you to make use of the print-to-video function of these programs which allow you to record your finished edit on to a connected digital video recorder or camera. As with importing video, you can connect the camera to the computer with a firewire lead and card.

Converting computer edits to video footage may be far from straightforward, largely because most of the equipment designed to do it is produced with television companies and production houses in mind and is consequently incredibly expensive. Equipment made for the casual home user is often not designed to do everything you require to produce your animated film. For instance, most digital video cameras sold in Britain have the record setting disabled, preventing you from taping your animation from a computer. There are a number of devices and plug-ins which will allow you to get around this problem; you can even order a camera from abroad. However, make sure that you always check the specification of any equipment you are using, and be prepared to search topical magazines and websites to get it to do exactly what you want.

Using the professionals Because of the complications involved in getting animation on video, and also because the equipment involved may be expensive and will be used for only a couple of days at the end of production, many people choose to get their video production done by a professional video editing company. Most freelance animators, and quite a few small animation companies, go down this route.

You do not have to use a large professional company used to producing television series and advertisements; most areas of the country will have a few small video companies with the equipment and expertise to help you. However, remember that these companies may not have had much experience with animation, so you will probably need to talk them through what you want. It is important to find out what format they will need your animation in. Most companies will be able to work with avi and QuickTime files, and some packages will accept swf files. However, some companies will prefer to use an image sequence, a series of files containing a separate image file for every frame of your movie. If you re using an image sequence you need to make sure that you use a good quality image format. Formats such as bitmaps, PNGs or TGAs all work well. But be wary of

Video Editing Software

If you want to put your animation on to video yourself, instead of using a professional company, you will need to get hold of some video editing software. The two best-known packages for doing this are Adobe Premier and Final Cut Pro. Premier will run only on Windows, and Final Cut Pro will run only on Macs. Both programs will let you edit your video and your sound, apply effects, add titles and output to video. Both will also give you a range of codecs options for outputting (codecs are the different ways of storing video imagery). This means that you will be able to export your animation for NTSC (the format for video in North America) and PAL (the format in Europe; *see* Chapter 5 for more on video formats). This is useful if you are planning to send your finished film to film festivals around the world. At the time of writing, both packages cost around $1,000. You will also need a fairly fast computer to run them; the technical specifications are listed below.

More affordable video editing programs do exist, although the cheapest are aimed squarely at the home video market and so are more suited to handling video footage of children's birthday parties than working with the intricate, frame-by-frame timings of animation. One cheaper package which is worth a try is Pinnacle Studio, which provides all the basic editing requirements, plus the option to buy specialist plug-ins for music, sound effects and special effects. While it is not as sophisticated as Premiere or Final Cut, it is more affordable; the main program tends to cost around $100. Another advantage of Pinnacle is that it is compatible with some of the Windows packages supplied with home PCs, such as Windows ME.

System Requirements

Adobe Premier	Microsoft Windows XP
	Intel Pentium III 800MHz processor
Final Cut Pro	Mac OS X v10.3.2 or later
	350MHz or faster PowerPC G4 or G5 processor
Pinnacle Studio	Windows 98SE, ME, 2000 or XP
	Intel Pentium or AMD Athlon 800MHz

As with all software, always make sure that your computer has the right specification before buying.

using any format designed to compress the file size, such as JPGs – the quality of the image will be reduced in compression, making your final film much less clear. Always have a quick look at any image sequence you have created to check the quality of the images.

As a general point, you need to take much more care when you are giving your film to someone else to transfer to video than when you are doing it yourself. You will spot mistakes in your film and will be able to replace them. A professional company will not necessarily know what your film is supposed to look like, and will have neither the time nor the inclination to correct any mistakes they do spot.

Drawn Animation

If you are using drawn animation, how you produce it will vary slightly according to how you are colouring it. You can colour your images by hand, using crayons, ink or even cel paint, or you can digitally colour them in a computer program. Either way, you will need to get your images into some video editing software to produce a finished version of your film. If you colour your images by hand, then you can film them on video and import them into your computer by using a firewire or analogue-to-digital conversion device. Alternatively, you could use a scanner to scan the coloured images into your computer.

If you are colouring images digitally then it is best to scan them into the computer. Professional companies use specialist animation colouring packages, such as Toonz or Animo, although the price of these puts them out of reach of the average individual film-maker. However, you can use conventional computer art programs such as Photoshop instead.

Film Animation

If you have shot your animation on film, then your editing will need to be done by hand rather than by using a computer. To do this you will need to get hold of a film and a tape splice and physically cut out bits of film and stick them together to produce a finished version. You will also need to have a projector so that you can show your finished film. As with all film equipment, it is most frequently found by searching websites and magazines for second-hand equipment made redundant by the computer age.

9   SHOWING YOUR FILM

Once you have made your film you will probably want to show it to people. For some, this will be a simple matter of making a few copies of it and passing them round to friends and family. Of course, this is absolutely fine – there is nothing wrong with making a film for no other reason than entertaining yourself and friends. However, some might want to take their film a step further. Having spent much time and effort on it, it might be that you want as many people as possible to see it. It might even be that you have decided that you want to make a career of animating and use your film to start that career. Alternatively, it could be that your film is a pilot for a television series and you want to show it to television and animation companies in the hope of it getting commissioned. In this final chapter we shall look at all these ways of using your finished film.

SHOWING YOUR FILM ON THE INTERNET

The internet has transformed the process of watching films; for little or no outlay your film can be seen by anyone with access to a computer and a modem. You can show it on your own personal website or submit it to specialist film and animation websites. In either case, there are some useful things you can do to encourage others to watch it.

Making Your Film Work on the Internet
The best way of getting your film to work well on the internet is to make it quick to download. No one likes sitting in front of a computer screen waiting; especially when they do not know whether the film they are waiting for will be any good. To keep your audience's waiting time to a minimum, you need to keep the file size of your film as small as possible. Some forms of animation are better suited to this than others; 2D computer animation can be very compact, especially when exported as a Flash player file (this format was especially designed for watching internet animation), but, by contrast, a QuickTime movie of a ten-minute-long stop-motion film will not be nearly so compact. You can reduce the image quality of a movie and its size on the screen, but, of course, this means that your film will not look quite as clear as it should do. It can be difficult to decide between showing a version of your film with a reduced quality but small file size, and a version with a better quality of picture which will take a long time to download. One common way of getting around this problem is to put two different versions of your film on-line: one for people accessing the internet with a slow dial-up connection and one for broadband users.

It is also important that your film's format is one which can be easily used (*see* Chapter 8 for more information on file formats). If you are showing your film on your personal website, it is a good idea to include a link allowing users to download the software needed to view your film.

Showing Your Film on a Personal Website

If you want to put your film on the internet yourself you will need three things: the website itself (including your film), software to upload it on to the internet and web space to load it into. Creating a simple website is fairly easy; there are several software packages which will create the necessary programming for you, but a good beginners' book on HTML, the language used to make web pages, should allow you to create a simple website quite easily. Web pages can be typed using any simple word processor, which means that, given time, you can create a good website without having to buy any new software.

Getting hold of web space to host your site should also be fairly easy. Most internet service providers (ISPs) give you a certain amount of web space free when you sign up to them. If you do not have a connection with an ISP at home, then it is easy to find free web hosts on the internet. However, remember that the web space will usually be free because it will be covered in advertisements and pop-up windows; it may be worth paying for a small amount for web space to avoid having too many advertisements on screen distracting users from your film.

Once you have created your website and secured your web space you need what is called file transfer protocol (FTP) software. This will let you upload your website on to your web space. FTP software is cheap and can easily be downloaded from the internet. If you have an ISP, check to see whether they recommend the use of a particular FTP program. Otherwise just go for something that is cheap and easy to use.

Other Websites for Showing Your Film

There are a number of film and animation websites which will show individual animators' films. Although they are unlikely to pay you for showing your film, they will provide a much higher potential audience for it, as well as taking care of the technical work needed to upload it. Before submitting your film to any of the websites listed below, or to any other sites, make sure that you are clear about what happens to the rights to your film. You want to make sure that the site is not demanding copyright over your film or its characters, so always read any agreements thoroughly before signing them.

New websites for showing films are appearing all the time (and often disappearing with the same frequency). However, the following sites are all recommended and used by many animators to show their films.

- Atom Films (www.atomfilms.com): based in the USA, Atom films are one of the largest hosts of animation on the internet. Their site gets millions of viewers a month and they are always looking for new films to showcase on it. Atom Films are interested in any film less than 30 minutes long.
- Reelmind (www.reelmind.com): this is a general film site with a large animation section. Registering with the site is free, and doing so will allow you to show up to 35 minutes of film, as well as giving you your own microsite.
- 10 Second Club (www.10secondclub. net): this site runs a monthly competition where animators are given a piece of

dialogue and produce character animation to go with it, with the best results being shown on the site. Although this means you cannot show your own film, it is a good way of practising your animation and getting it seen.

SHOWING YOUR FILM AT FESTIVALS

Another way of getting people to see your film is to show it at film festivals. The obvious advantages of doing this – it is possible to win prizes and get yourself known – are matched by some major disadvantages. The first of these is that it can be difficult to get your film into a festival since each will have only a limited number of places available. Everyone can show his or her film on the internet, but only a few can fit into a 90-minute programme of films at a festival. Another problem is money: you will often have to pay a fee to enter your film in a competition. It might not be much, but if you are entering several festivals the costs soon add up.

However, do not let these disadvantages put you off. Getting your film into a festival is exciting, and you never know who will see it there or what will happen. You could win some very useful prizes – many festival competitions give money or film equipment to the winners – and, at the very least, you will have an interesting holiday. It is important to research any festival that you are thinking of entering; make sure that your film meets the festival's requirements and be honest with yourself about your chances of being accepted. If most of the previous winners seem to have several Oscars to their name, then it might not be the place to show your first film.

New animation festivals, and film festivals with animation sections, are springing up all the time, and so the list below is by no means exhaustive. However, it gives an indication of the range of locations and formats that festivals take place in.

- Annecy International Animated Film Festival (www.annecy.org): often referred to simply as 'Annecy' after the French town that hosts it, this is the most prestigious animation festival in the world. As well as categories such as best short film, best feature and best television series, there are also awards for best short film and best student film. The standard of competition is very high.
- Animated Encounters: The Bristol International Animation Festival (www.animated-encounters.org.uk): the biggest animation festival in Britain, Animated Encounters is sponsored by several large television channels, and so tends to concentrate on professional work ahead of arty, personal films.
- Ottawa International Animation Festival (www.awn.com/ottawa): probably the biggest animation festival in North America, this is set to merge with the International Student Animation Festival of Ottawa and will include a special section for student films.
- The Australian International Animation Festival (www.miaf.net): this starts as the Melbourne International Animation Festival, before the programme of events switches to Sydney and becomes the Australian International Animation Festival. Although large parts of the festival concentrate on showing classic films from animation history, it does accept entries of new films every year.
- Anima (www.awn.com/folioscope): this big international festival takes place in Brussels and combines talks and screenings by famous names in animation with

films from young up and coming animators.

- Fantoche International Animation Film Festival (www.fantoche.ch): a smaller, less business-like festival in Switzerland.
- The Animation Show (www.animation-show.com): this festival tours round cinemas in North America instead of being based in a city. It aims to showcase the best in short animated films and welcomes submissions from students as well as professionals.
- Bradford Animation Festival (www.baf.org.uk): based at the National Museum of Photography, Film and Television in Bradford, the festival has a special category for non-professional films.
- Holland Animation Film Festival (www.awn.com/haff): a biennial festival based in Utrecht. The festival is split between 'Applied Animation' and 'Independent Animation' (another way of describing the difference between professional and personal films).

SHOWING YOUR FILM TO COMPANIES

If you want animation companies or television channels to produce a series based on your film or to invest in another of your ideas, you will need to show your film to them. Showing your film to these companies is not as hard to do as you might think; all companies are looking for the next big success and will be prepared to see anyone who thinks they have a good idea. However, these companies will often have hundreds of people wanting to show them their films, so you need to approach them in the right way to ensure that they pay attention to your film.

When it comes to approaching a company it is very important to do your own research first. Try to find out about the kind of animation the company makes; this will save you from trying to interest 3D animation companies in your pilot for a cut-out animation series, or approaching Hollywood film studios with your 30-second web animation. Also make sure that you know the right person to talk to. It is not always obvious who this may be; in some companies it may be the art director, in others the head of production or the chief animator. Different companies work in different ways; if you are not sure of the best person to approach, call the company up and ask.

Once you have got hold of the right people at the right company, see whether it is possible to show them your film in person. This has the advantage of making sure that they actually watch it, and it also gives you the chance to ask questions and get feedback. Of course, it is not always possible to do this; you might live hundreds of miles away from the company or just not manage to find a time when the right person is free. In such instances you will need to send them a tape. Before doing this, talk to the person you are sending the tape to and check that he or she is happy for you to do so. If they agree, address the tape to that particular person and include a letter saying that you are posting your film as requested. This should avoid your film ending up on the pile of unwatched films and show reels which sit in the corner of all animation studios.

Remember that only a small number of animated television series and professional films are made each year, so do not be too disappointed if your film or idea is not commissioned, but make sure that you take on board any constructive feedback that you are given, and that your next film is even better.

OTHER WAYS OF SHOWING YOUR FILM

If you live in a city where a number of animation companies are based or where there is an art school teaching animation you will often find bars or cafés running animation film nights where several films are shown in a short programme. As well as getting people to see your film, this can be a good way of meeting other animators (which is useful if you are looking for someone to help on your next film).

It may be hard to find out about these small screenings, particularly if you are not studying or working in animation. In Britain it is possible to stay up to date with events by registering with Shooting People (http://shootingpeople.org) who produce a twice-weekly bulletin with news on festivals, screenings, jobs, work experience and almost everything else of relevance. Shooting People also produces an American bulletin, although at the moment it really encompasses only New York. Outside the United Kingdom the best international resource for animation news is Animation World Network (www.awn.com), which contains a huge amount of information. It also produces a weekly email newsletter.

TAKING THINGS FURTHER

Once you have completed your film you will realize quite how much hard work animation involves, and also, one hopes, how enjoyable it can be. If all that work has not put you off, it is possible that you will want to take things further and to work professionally in animation.

If that is your aim, you need to first focus on exactly what it is you want to do. Think about the parts of the film-making process which you got most satisfaction from, the things you are best at doing. You could be an animator, a director or a scriptwriter. If what you liked best was co-ordinating the whole project, then you could be a producer.

Once you know what it is you want to do, there are two options open to you. You could study your subject academically or you could look for professional work straightaway. If you can spare the time and money, taking a suitable course is always a good idea; as well as teaching you new skills, it will also give you the time to produce a bigger range of work to show to prospective employers. Studying script writing or animation will allow you to try different styles of work and to experiment with new ideas, something that can be hard to do in a professional environment where you will need to take any work you can get. You do not necessarily have to do a full degree course; many colleges run shorter length ones which can still be useful.

If you want to get straight into professional work you will need to be prepared to start very low. Lots of animation companies employ runners who act as general dogsbodies; they make the tea, run errands, do photocopying and, occasionally, help with animation. The pay is always low, but it can provide a good opportunity to get started in animation. If you want to be a runner, try to combine looking for work with showing companies your film. If you are lucky and your film really impresses a company, they might offer you work as an animator. If they do not, which is the more likely outcome, ask them whether they employ runners and what you need to do to be employed as one.

If you are thinking of working in animation you will have to allow a certain amount of realism into your thoughts. Making your own film is a very idealistic activity; you can do whatever you want to for as long as you are prepared to spend the time needed to do it. Professional animation will have a much bigger budget than your personal film, but, more often than not, will give you fewer options, so you will need to be flexible. For example, you may have decided that, although you enjoyed animating your film, what you would really like to do is character design. The problem with this is that an average television series might employ twenty animators, but only one character designer. Animation work is sometimes in short supply and is almost always paid on a freelance or contract basis, so it is best to be able to do as much as possible. Mix character design with animation or directing with storyboarding, and be prepared to work on films or series with different styles of animation and different levels of quality.

If professional animation sounds somewhat daunting, then don't worry. Remember that animation is meant to be enjoyable; there are many serious jobs in the world, but making cartoons is definitely not one of them. There is nothing wrong with continuing to dabble with making personal films in your spare time and to keep animation as an enjoyable hobby, just as there is nothing wrong with trying to make a living from something you enjoy. But whatever you do with your animation, the most important thing is to have fun.

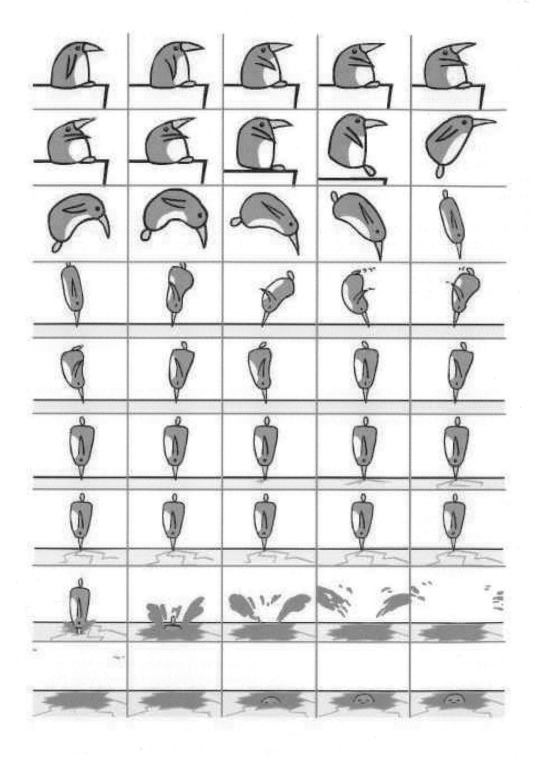

FILMOGRAPHY

This is a list of all the animated films and television series referred to in the book. It shows the date they were first shown and the people or company who made them.

Television Series

2DTV (2DTV, 2001)
The Big Knights (Astley Baker, 1999)
Creature Comforts (Aardman Animation, 1988)
Dangermouse (Cosgrove Hall, 1980)
The Flintstones (Hanna-Barbera, 1960)
Henry's Cat (Stan Hayward and Bob Godfrey Films, 1982)
King of the Hill (Fox, 1997)
The Magic Roundabout (Danot Enterprises, 1965)
Monkeydust (BBC, 2002).
Monty Python's Flying Circus (BBC, 1969)
Morph (Aardman Animation, for the BBC, 1978)
Mr Benn (Zephyr Film Productions, 1971)
Mr Magoo (UPA Films, 1949)
Pigeon Street (David Yates, for the BBC, 1981)
Pugwash (BBC, 1973)
Roobarb and Custard (Grange Calveley, 1974)
Scooby Doo (Hanna-Barbera, 1969)
The Simpsons (Fox, 1987)
South Park (Trey Parker and Matt Stone, 1997)
Tom and Jerry (MGM, 1939)
Top Cat (Hanna-Barbera, 1961)
Wallace and Gromit (Aardman Animation, 1989)
Yogi Bear (Hanna-Barbera, 1958)

Feature Films
Disney
Snow White and the Seven Dwarfs (1937)
Fantasia (1940)
Pinocchio (1940)
Saludos Amigos (1942)
The Three Caballeros (1944)
The Jungle Book (1967)

Pixar
Toy Story (1995)
Toy Story 2 (1999)
Monsters, Inc. (2001)
Finding Nemo (2003)

Studio Ghibli
My Neighbour Totoro (1988)
Princess Mononoke (1997).
Spirited Away (2001).

Dreamworks
Antz (1998)
Chicken Run (with Aardman Animation, 2000)
Shrek (2001)

Other Companies
Who Framed Roger Rabbit? (Touchstone, 1988)
Belleville Rendezvous (co-produced by eighteen companies, including Canal+, Téléfilm Canada and the BBC, 2003)
Akira (Akira Committee Company, 1988)

Short Films
Alice (co-produced by several European companies, including Channel Four Films and Condor Films, 1987)
The Big Snitt (National Film Board of Canada, 1985)
The Cat Came Back (National Film Board of Canada, 1988)
Father and Daughter (CinéTé Filmproductie BV and Cloudrunner, 2000)
Gertie the Dinosaur (Winsor McCay, 1918)
Humorous Phases of Funny Faces (Stuart Blackton, 1906)
Leonardo's Diary (Studio Jiriho Trnky, 1972)

Little Nemo in Slumberland (Winsor McCay, 1911)

Looney Tunes (Warner Brothers, 1930)

Luxo Jnr. (Pixar, 1986)

The Monk and the Fish (Folimage Valence Production, 1994)

The Sinking of the Lusitania (Winsor McCay, 1918)

Steamboat Willie (Disney, 1928)

The Street (National Film Board of Canada, 1976)

BIBLIOGRAPHY

Animation

Blair, Preston, *Cartoon Animation (The Collectors' Series)* (Walter Foster Art Books, 1995)

Maestri, George, *Digital Character Animation* (New Rider's Publishing, 1996)

Roberts, Steve, *Character Animation in 3D* (Focal Press Visual Effects and Animation, 2004)

Shaw, Susannah, *Stop Motion: Craft Skills for Model Animation* (Focal Press Visual Effects and Animation, 2003)

Whitaker, Harold, and Halas, John, *Timing for Animation* (Focal Press Ltd, 1981)

White, Tony, *The Animator's Workshop* (Watson-Guptill Publications, 1988)

Williams, Richard, *The Animator's Survival Kit* (Faber and Faber, 2002)

Industry Handbooks

Animation UK (BECTU, publishing annually)

AWN Global Animation Business Directory (AWN, published annually)

Other Useful Books

Muybridge, Eadweard, *Animals in Motion* (Dover Books, 1989)

Muybridge, Eadweard, *The Human Figure in Motion* (Dover Books, 1989)

Postgate, Oliver, *Seeing Things: An Autobiography* (Pan Macmillan, 2000)

Schneider, Steve, *That's All Folks: The Art of Warner Bros* (Barnes and Noble, 1988)

Thomas, Frank and Johnson, Ollie, *The illusion of life – Disney Animation* (Disney Editions, 1995)

SUPPLIERS

It can be hard to track down specialist animation equipment, such as peg bars or dope sheets. The following is a list of equipment suppliers.

United Kingdom

Paper People,
Slade Farm
Morechard Bishop
Crediton
Devon EX17 6SJ
01363 850850;
www.paperpeople.co.uk

Chromacolour
Unit 5
Pilton Estate
Croydon
CR0 3RA
020 8688 1991;
www.chromacolour.co.uk

United States

Cartoon Supplies
36125 Travis Ct
Temecula
CA 92592
+ 909-693-5086;
www.cartoonsupplies.com

INDEX